NASCAR
WOMEN

NASCAR WOMEN

DENISE WOOD

DAVID BULL PUBLISHING

Library of Congress Control Number: 2003106288

ISBN: 1 893618 31 5

NASCAR is a registered trademark of the National Association for Stock Car Auto Racing.

David Bull Publishing, logo, and colophon are trademarks of David Bull Publishing, Inc.

Book and cover design: Anna Gilbert, Blue Design, Portland, Maine

Printed in the United States

10 9 8 7 6 5 4 3 2 1

David Bull Publishing
4250 East Camelback Road
Suite K150
Phoenix, AZ 85018

602-852-9500
602-852-9503 (fax)

www.bullpublishing.com

Author photo: Bob Brown

Table of Contents

Acknowledgments

First I must thank the women in this book: Nancy, Debbie, Gail, Danielle, Lesa, Katie, Arlene, Andrea, Jackie, Pattie, Buffy, Stevie, and Deb. Obviously without them this book would not exist, but I am so grateful for the incredible generosity of time and spirit that they all offered me. They allowed me to invade their privacy, spend many hours with them in their motor homes, and pester them with phone calls throughout the writing and editing process.

Special thanks and much appreciation go out to Jim Hunter and Tish Sheets, without whom this project may have ended prematurely. With their help and unwavering enthusiasm, it became bigger and better.

To David Bull for taking a chance on a former journalist who had never tackled a project this big before. And for making me work and rework each chapter so that each profile would be the best that it could be.

I also owe a great deal to Steve and Melody Rose. Thank you for your wonderful photos and for constantly digging through your archives to meet my never-ending requests.

Thanks to Montgomery Lee Petty and her trainer Stacy Hullett for allowing me to tag along to the East Coast National Horse Show. And to all of the public relations people who helped relay messages, gather photos, and get me in touch with the women.

Opposite: Team owner Gail Davis calls motorcycle riding one of the great joys of her life. She and husband Bill are regulars on Kyle Petty's Charity Ride across the country. Here she takes a break during a fuel stop on what has become known as Kyle's Ride. (Gail Davis collection)

DAYTONA
500
DAYTONA
INTERNATIONAL SPEEDWAY
DAYTONA
NATIONAL SPEEDWAY
Series
NASCAR
NAPA
NAPA
SIMPSON
CHAMPION
NAPA
AUTO PARTS
NAPA
AutoCare
CENTER
AUTO PARTS

Introduction

Glamorous and exciting.

A life filled with money, travel, and celebrities.

We have all viewed with envy the lives of movie stars on the red carpet and professional sports figures jet-setting around the country. That same spotlight has caught the world of NASCAR in its glare, and while the camera helps create celebrity, it often distorts our perceptions of both the life and the individuals in it.

The spotlight once shined exclusively on the NASCAR driver, but now seems to shine more and more brightly on the driver's wife with each passing week. The camera follows her as she walks in a relaxed manner down pit road trying to ignore its ever-present intrusion. It watches intently as she unabashedly sheds tears when her husband makes his way to victory lane for the first time.

The increased exposure of the sport has also popularized women in the business and media areas of NASCAR, and has made a variety of career opportunities available to women that did not exist a decade ago. While many on the outside perceive a job in racing as all fun and games, by reading the profiles of the women in this book you will discover that this is far from the case. Through the years, more and more women have chosen to entrench themselves in this arena on a professional level. They work hard to be taken seriously as women in a so-called man's domain.

Many of the women involved in NASCAR are drivers' wives. They time laps during practice and help calculate fuel mileage on race day. They keep the books back at home and handle appearance schedules. They also raise their children on the road and attempt to maintain some sense of normality for their families. They do all of this, despite the fact that they are constantly in the public eye and some of their faces can be found on cereal

Opposite: Michael Waltrip finally answered the question of when he would win a Winston Cup points race. He earned his first triumph in the 2001 Daytona 500, where he celebrated in victory lane with Buffy. (Steven Rose/MMP, Inc)

boxes or in advertisements.

Other women who make the sport tick include car owner Gail Davis, who with her husband, Bill, has built one of the most impressive Winston Cup organizations and facilities in racing. There's Lesa France Kennedy, the third-generation France who orchestrated the development and construction of Kansas Speedway and is president of International Speedway Corporation. Another woman, Jackie Pegram, began the children's ministry with Motor Racing Outreach and made it blossom into something the NASCAR family now can not imagine being without.

My own involvement with racing began as a journalist in 1989 with *The Richmond Times-Dispatch* in Richmond, Virginia, and the *Virginian-Pilot* in Norfolk, Virginia. I became a sponsor public relations representative for Sports Marketing Enterprises in 1995. I have also done public relations work for RCA and Roush Racing. In the winter of 2000, I married James Ince, crew chief of the MBV Pontiac driven by Johnny Benson. I have seen the sport from several different perspectives.

I knew some of the women in this book well before I began to write it, but others I was meeting for the first time. As I began spending more time with each of them, I discovered that the ways in which they help the sport pale in comparison to what remarkable women they are. I also grew to understand that there is not a racing wife out there—whether she is married to a driver, crew chief, or tire changer—who has not felt that she plays second fiddle to the business that Debbie Benson refers to as a "disease, not a sport." NASCAR Winston Cup racing is not a job to the drivers, it is a life, and at times an obsession. For most it is all that they know; the notion of "leaving the office at the office" is just not possible. More times than not, the wife's home life is directly affected by how things are going at the racetrack. Winning truly is everything.

The core racing community is a small, tightly knit group. The life is an odd one. Thursdays are spent traveling. The rest of the weekend is spent racing before returning home Sunday night after the race, only to get up Monday morning and prepare to do it all again. If you ever catch a glimpse of your neighbors at home, you are lucky, but finding time to get to know them is difficult at best. NASCAR is your neighborhood, and it's the neighborhood of your children, thirty-six weekends a year.

The garage opens early every morning of the weekend, as early as 6:00 a.m. on race day. As the crew members file into the garage, so too do the public relations representatives and reporters, and none of their jobs are complete when the garage closes. It is then that stories are filed and public appearances scheduled.

Motor Racing Outreach is an organization that provides continuity for families in this pell-mell environment. Perhaps the most important thing MRO offers to everyone in the community is an understanding of this indescribably difficult life and someone to talk to

about life at any time. You will notice a lot of references to MRO in the pages of this book. It has become a part of the life, "the glue that holds us all together," says Ann Schrader.

In the three years that I have spent putting this book together, I have seen the women on the following pages go through tremendous tragedy and find incredible joy, sometimes at nearly the same instant. I was often impressed by the openness with which these women shared their emotions.

Adam Petty was alive when this project began, and my first interview with Pattie, his mother, was at Texas Motor Speedway on the weekend of his Winston Cup debut. I saw Buffy Waltrip share the elation and unbelievable pain of her husband, Michael's, first Winston Cup triumph at the same time that his car owner, Dale Earnhardt, was killed in a crash in turn four of the 2001 Daytona 500. I listened as Stevie Waltrip reminisced about long-ago days on the racetrack that were fun and the recent years that have been anything but fun.

A not-yet 21-year-old Katie Kenseth spoke unsurely about herself. Still new to racing and freshly engaged, she was unable to hide the overwhelming feelings that being thrown into this community can often bring. She has since blossomed into a very confident, but still quiet, young woman, much wiser than her years.

Lesa Kennedy sat relaxed and offered a rare interview just hours before the start of the Daytona 500. She admitted she hardly ever grants interviews, yet she made me feel at ease and answered questions freely.

These women live extraordinary lives. They deal with unimaginable stresses with a strength and courage that is to be admired. And they relish their challenges.

I hope you will see that these are very real women. I think that is what they want you to see, too.

Goody's
BODY PAIN
FORMULA
STP
STP
GAS
TREATMENT
FREE
25% MORE
STP
SON
OF A
GUN!
Protectant
PONTIAC
NASCAR
Winston Cup
Series
PLAYERS
INC
spree
prepaid card
STP
Racing
STP
MARTINSVILLE
Speedway

NANCY ANDRETTI

John Andretti pulled the STP Pontiac into victory lane at Martinsville Speedway on April 18, 1999. It was the second win of Andretti's Winston Cup career and the first since his return to the seat of the famed Petty Enterprises No. 43 Pontiac. He fought from one lap down with a two-tire stop to take the lead from Jeff Burton with four laps to go, and he never looked back.

Andretti climbed wearily from the car. Cameras were rolling, microphones were not quite in position, but there was no mistaking the first words from his mouth.

"Where's Nancy?"

Andretti's wife of thirteen years was making her way through the crowd as quickly as she could. John grabbed her and pulled her close before allowing the interviewing to begin. To observers it was a sweet moment between a husband and a wife. It was a moment that accompanies the end of every race weekend, only the drivers' and wives' names change. But for John and Nancy it was so much more.

Although it was John's second trip to victory lane, it had been nearly two years since his first win at Daytona, in July 1997, driving the No. 98 RCA-sponsored Ford. Since that first win the pair had weathered the termination of RCA's involvement in racing and the upheaval of an entire team. John ultimately returned to Petty Enterprises, the team that he had spent some of his early Winston Cup days with and the place he had always felt the most at home. Now John and Nancy had finally found their way back to victory lane.

"My dad was at that race," Nancy says. "We had been through so much together and that win came after my mother had passed away. When you go through [the death of a family member] you bond in a different way."

John and Nancy's bond had survived the normal trials and tribulations of racing in both CART and NASCAR. "It's the same everywhere. It is difficult to lose a ride or a sponsor no matter where you are," Nancy says.

Add to that the adjustment of making a life in Charlotte, North Carolina, far from their home in Indianapolis, Indiana, and the tragedy of watching Nancy's mother succumb to cancer the previous fall. "He was there when I was crying myself to sleep at night, every night. You wonder if the pain is ever going to get better. It was hard for him because he didn't know what to do for me because at the time he had never lost anyone in his family, not even a close friend."

"I have to be honest with you," John told her. "I don't know what to do for you, what to say. What is the right thing to do or say?" Nancy assured John there was no right or wrong thing, but he was always there for her to lean on just as she has been there for him. They have one of those marriages that is a true partnership.

After a practice or qualifying session you are just as likely to hear Nancy asking about the car as you are the crew chief. And John doesn't just hand out the pat answers he would to someone who doesn't know much about cars. Nancy gets the full story. She is told

about the shocks, the springs, the track bar, just as if she were one of the crew. If Nancy has a comment, John listens with interest.

"I have always grilled him. Every day after he comes home I grill him. Kim [Burton, Jeff's wife] and I do the same thing, she calls it the debriefing. 'How was the car?' 'What happened after the last pit stop, you just went back.' 'Why didn't they do this?' 'Why didn't they do that?'

"He trusts me. He knows I'm really interested. He knows I care about what happens. It's not that I could do anything to help them or fix the car or anything like that, but we have just always had that kind of relationship where he would just tell me. We are the only two that know everything we have been through throughout his career. He's close with his dad, but even his dad hasn't been there like I have."

Born Nancy Summers in 1963 in Indianapolis, Nancy was the seventh of eight kids—four boys and four girls—born to Lois and Carl Summers. She grew up with strong Catholic faith instilled by not only her parents but also twelve years of Catholic school.

"It was very important to my mom and dad for us to go to Catholic school. To send us each through school for twelve years, it was very expensive for them, but they did it because they

thought it was the right thing to do."

Despite being busy raising eight children, Lois Summers wanted to work outside the home. Carl, who spent forty years at General Motors, agreed that if she could find a job that still afforded her time to be with the kids, then she could do it. For twenty years, Lois worked in the hardware department at Sears from 9:00 a.m. to 1:00 p.m., and loved it. "She used her money to buy curtains and stuff for the house," Nancy says. That enabled Carl to use his income to feed and educate the kids. "Money wasn't important to him and that was one of the things he wanted to instill in us."

The relationship between Nancy and John began during the summer of 1982 when John returned home to Indianapolis in between semesters at Moravian College in Pennsylvania. Nancy Summers' phone started to ring and ring and ring. "John kept asking me out," Nancy laughs. "I kept saying 'no.'

"You can say we knew each other in high school. It was a small school, so we knew who each other was, but we didn't date then. We didn't really have the same circle of friends. I was into sports and student council. John would go to school and then go home and work on his race cars. That was his deal."

John's sister and Nancy were both cheerleaders in school and occasionally she would give Nancy a ride home, but that was really all the contact Nancy ever had with John.

PENNZOIL
HALL/VDS Racing
PPG
PENNZOIL
BELL
PENNZOIL
BELL
John Andretti
Y CAR
SERIES
GOLD COAST
PRIX

And despite growing up in Indianapolis, Nancy had attended just one Indy 500 with some friends while she was in high school. It was far from a life-altering experience for her.

"I didn't really have any interest in it," she says.

But it wasn't racing that caused Nancy to continually turn down John's requests for dates. "I was dating someone else, he happened to be named John too. They both knew about it, but John Andretti kept calling. Finally my mother told me I should just go out with him so he would stop calling." Fortunately for John, Nancy listened to her mother.

Once Nancy got to know John and spend time with him, it was hard to avoid developing at least some interest in racing, but even then it was minimal. To build and maintain a relationship at the same time John was building his racing career was a challenge.

To meet the scheduling demands, John and Nancy set up a regular date each week. "I was wondering if you want to go to the dirt track races tonight," John once asked hopefully.

"No, that's not where I want to go for our date," Nancy said.

John was somewhat dumbfounded. "Well, I'm going with some friends and I really thought you might want to go. Let's do that for our date."

More than a little bit annoyed that John really expected her to spend their date night at a racetrack with his friends, Nancy gave a firm, and potentially final, no.

"I told him not to call me anymore after that. It took him a long time to get back in my good graces," Nancy says, smiling. "I did not take that well. He chose racing over me and he wasn't getting paid for it. He was just going to spectate. That really bothered me." That was just the beginning. Getting involved with a racer takes some getting used to.

John and Nancy dated for nearly four years before becoming engaged, but a couple of years before the engagement Nancy had quit her job as a customer service representative for Blue Cross/Blue Shield and her studies at Indiana University-Purdue University at Indianapolis. She had been following a general course study, although she had some interest in respiratory therapy due to her own struggles with asthma and allergies. Nancy has a severe gluten allergy, which prevents her from eating wheat and many yeast products, and was diagnosed with asthma shortly after she started dating John.

"John's family had cats and I'd never been exposed to cats. When I went over to his house for the first time I just about had an asthma attack. I just couldn't handle it," Nancy says. John took her to the allergist and made sure she had every test possible. "He even paid for all of the tests that night. I couldn't afford it. I'd never felt better than I did after we had all of that done." Nancy finally understood her allergies and was able to treat them.

The decision to leave school and work wasn't a difficult one for her. "I wasn't really established in a career yet, so that helped. And I knew that we were going to want to have children once we got married, and the plan had always been for me to stay home. I just felt very fortunate that we were able to afford for me to stay home and take care of the kids."

But make no mistake, Nancy has always helped out with the race team as much as possible. "I used to keep track of all of John's times and talk to the pit board guy and tell him the times to put on the pit board and the lap to pit on. When we made the move to Charlotte, I told John I'd like to find something so that I could stay involved. So I've kept lap times for him for every team he has been with."

She glances at her swollen belly. "Now with two kids and one on the way, I'm as involved as I want to be right now." She may not have been helping out with lap times during practice sessions with the new baby on the way, but she could still be found clocking laps on race day up until the final month of her pregnancy with Amelia, their third child.

Others may not believe it, but there are times when it is easy to forget that the life she leads is not exactly normal and her husband is not just a working dad. Then there are little reminders. "Hey Mom, Andrew said that he had breakfast with my dad today," her 7-year-old son, Jarett, announced when Nancy retrieved him from school one afternoon in 2000. Completely baffled, she asked him what he was talking about.

"Well, he was on the back of the cereal box. Isn't that funny?" Jarett said. Nancy agreed and laughed—she had forgotten that John's picture, adorned the packaging of Cheerios and other General Mills products. She herself has been featured on packages of Hamburger Helper, which one of Jarett's teachers had recognized that same week. "I hate the picture," Nancy says. "But they didn't have those boxes up in Indiana for a long time and my family wanted them so bad I had to get a bunch and send them up there."

It wasn't that long ago that Jarett thought that since his dad was on television all the time, everyone was. One Saturday afternoon the entire family went to watch Nancy's nephew play football. It was a 5A high school state championship game being played in the RCA Dome in Indianapolis.

The next day, an NFL Sunday, the family's TV was tuned in to a game. "Is Justin going to be on today? Is that him?" Jarett asked.

Jarett and his sister Olivia were featured in a television ad for NASCAR that began airing in 1999. There have been times in restaurants when the fans interrupting the Andretti's dinner were seeking Olivia's autograph as well as John's.

"She just smiles and laughs," Nancy says. "Jarett gets annoyed when people ask for John's autograph at inappropriate times, like when we are eating. He won't be rude in front of the people but when they walk away, he'll say, 'Geez dad, we can't even eat a meal.' So at seven years old he is very aware of what is going on and what is and isn't appropriate."

There is no way around the fact that the life the Andrettis lead is far from what most of the world considers normal. But it has been through Jarett's schooling that Nancy has been able to find some normality not only for her children's life, but her own.

Nancy met a lot of people when Jarett began preschool and she has remained close with that group of women. "We have moms' night out once a month. I don't know what it was but that group formed a real bond, the adults and the children."

Jarett's best friend is from that group. In fact, Jarett chose not to attend the Darlington race in the spring of 2000 because he and his friend had a soccer game that weekend and he didn't want to miss it.

"Strangely enough, most of the people in his preschool were mostly transplants [to Charlotte] and mostly Catholic," Nancy says. "I found a real commonality with them. We'd go to McDonald's after the kids got out of school, we'd go to the park. Then when they graduated from preschool we were all sad. So we started this moms' night out and we stay in touch that way."

With their third child due in just a couple of months, Nancy's face radiates with beauty and peace. It's Saturday morning and she has yet to shower and change out of her pajamas. As Nancy fixes a bowl of grits for herself, Olivia has settled in front of the television for a morning of cartoon watching with her buddy Paige Burton—daughter of Jeff and Kim—who spent the night last night. Sounds like a typical family Saturday morning. And it is, for the Andrettis and most racing families. But in just a few moments, the reminder of how different their Saturday mornings are from the rest of the world's roars to life. Just several feet away from the sanctuary of the motor home, John hits the track at Darlington for Saturday morning's Winston Cup practice session.

Nancy and John haven't spent all of their time in a plush motor home. In fact, it really hasn't been that long that they even have been able to bring the children to the racetrack and have a place for them to be. Motor Racing Outreach changed all of that.

"We didn't have a motor home when we first came down here. The first year John raced, we stayed in seedy hotels with Jarett and the baby [Olivia]. Now it is much more family oriented here than in CART."

But that didn't make the transition from Indy to NASCAR any easier. "I don't know how to say it. The whole lifestyle and the way you are raised is different. In the South hardly anybody is Catholic and in the north everybody is Catholic. So I found I had less in common with people here."

The most difficult part for Nancy was, of course, watching John go through the school of hard knocks to earn his spot in Winston Cup racing. Neither will ever forget his first race. It was at North Wilkesboro, and John got hit by everybody on the track. "I knew he could handle it and all that, but you just don't want to see somebody you love kicked around like that. But that's all part of it."

At the 1999 Las Vegas race, John's engine let go during qualifying and he was forced to take a provisional starting spot for the first time in nearly two seasons. When teammate Kyle Petty had his engine blow that same day, the mood was far from pleasant in the Petty Enterprises camp.

Everyone was upset, and Nancy certainly felt bad as well, like you do when a loved one has a particularly rough day at the office. A comment was made by someone in the Petty organization that they were surprised she was doing as well as she was. "I looked up and, not being rude, but just matter-of-fact, said, 'You know what? There's other things in life besides racing.'"

There was a time when a blown engine would have seemed a lot more devastating to Nancy than it was on that day. But November 18, 1998, everything had changed.

One day in August of that year, Nancy was making the usual preparations for the weekend's race, the night race at Bristol Motor Speedway in Tennessee. The first of the two phone calls that would alter her life came.

"My mother had been diagnosed with cancer."

Without hesitation, Nancy scrapped her plans to go to Bristol, and headed home with the children to Indiana to be with her parents and seven brothers and sisters. It was the first race of John's she had missed in years. Nancy would make the trip between Charlotte and Indianapolis four times between August and November.

"It's never enough," she says, with tears she has no intention of apologizing for in her eyes. "You always have regrets. I wish I would have just said forget the racing, forget it all. John told me to do whatever I wanted to do as far as staying in Indy for a while, or whatever I needed. The kids were in school, so I was really torn."

The final call came from one of her sisters on Monday, November 16. The downward turn had begun in earnest. Her mother was in the hospital. The outlook was poor at best.

Nancy was on the first plane out of Charlotte.

She set up vigil at the hospital by her mother's side. Family members came and went and joined her, then as visiting hours came to a close, Nancy was alone with her mom.

"You can't stay here," the nurse told her.

Nancy refused to leave. "I'm spending the night. Someone has got to stay with her."

Realizing she was fighting a losing battle with this petite, determined woman, the nurse relented. "I won't tell you not to, just know that you're not allowed and be quiet. Try not to leave the room."

Not a problem, Nancy thought. She remained fixed to the edge of her mother's bed among the cold sterile machines and watched as her world was slowly, irreversibly altered with every breath her mother struggled to take. Each one drew her closer to her last.

The moaning began in the early morning hours.

"Mom, are you in pain?" Nancy asked, at the same time beckoning the nurse to administer more morphine.

"No, I'm OK."

"Mom, if you're in pain, tell me. I'll take care of you."

The nurse gave her more morphine, but the effect was unnoticeable. Her mother was up all night.

Finally, at around 5:00 a.m., the pain ended. Lois passed away.

"I was the only one with her. It all happened so quickly from the time she was diagnosed. We went over all the treatment options. She didn't want chemotherapy, she said she didn't want to lose her hair. We just ran out of time. It was all so quick." Nancy's eyes fill again. She makes a half-hearted attempt to wipe them, opting instead to place a hand on the swell of her tummy, the tears unable to dim her pregnant glow.

"That's why in Vegas I was able to keep my perspective. I'm going to have a baby and it's going to be healthy and we already have two great kids. I have a great marriage. I don't care about a blown motor. I felt for John, but it's not going to ruin me. It's not going to crush me.

"In this business it is very hard to keep your perspective, but things change. Your whole perspective on life changes after something like that happens."

Below: When Nancy gave birth to a baby girl in the spring of 2000, there was no question she would be named for Nancy's mother Lois. Nancy and Amelia Lois are shown here in March 2001. (Nancy Andretti collection)

CHAMPIONS
Lipton
24 FAMILY SIZE
TEA BAGS • 1 BAG MAKES 4 SERVINGS
Naturally Refreshing Iced Tea Blend
FRISK Tea
BUSCH
NET WT. 6 oz (170g)
Lipton TEA
GOODYEAR
Goody's
Johnny Benson Jr.
Lipton TEA
CHAMPION
NASCAR
BUSCH
BEER
SERIES
Grand National Division
1995
JOHNNY BENSON

Debbie Benson

Debbie Benson played basketball, softball, and volleyball in school, so when she was asked to fill in on her husband's pit crew one night, well, it just seemed normal.

"To me it was just like another sport I could do," Debbie says.

Johnny's father usually held the signboard on his ASA pit crew, but he was unable to attend one night, so crew chief Dave Taylor asked Debbie to do it. It turned into more than a one-night gig.

"The first couple of years we were racing, the sign board wasn't on a stick. You carried the sign out onto pit road and waved the cars in. ASA didn't have a pit road speed limit. I remember one night the crew chief kept telling me to go out a little bit farther, so I was just doing what I was told. After a couple of pit stops the official comes over to me and says, 'Honey, you've got to move in a little bit, you're in Mike's way.' I realized then that the crew chief was sending me out there so the competitor had to turn around me to get into his pit stall. I was like, 'Oh, thanks.'"

But Debbie carried the sign board for two years during Johnny's ASA career, and even did so during his first year of Busch Series racing in 1994.

"There were three girls on that ASA team. We figured, us girls travel to the racetrack anyway. So why bring an extra man to do the job? The crew chief's wife did the catch can and a friend of the family came along and she carried a tire. The tires weren't nearly as heavy as [Winston Cup] tires. I could pick up two tires and carry them back. That first year we did it, we never won a pit-stop competition, but we beat everyone out of the pits. The next year we won the pit stop competitions too. They did little interviews at the track and gave out trophies and stuff. Of course we took all the credit!"

Prior to those days, Debbie had never really considered herself a race fan, but

Johnny's father, Johnny Benson Sr., was a local star in Grand Rapids, Michigan, and her cousins were very into racing. She would reluctantly tag along to the track with them to watch, but never really knew anything about it.

One of Johnny Jr.'s best friends was her cousin, and she and Johnny had known of one another since elementary school.

"He is three years older than me and we just ran in two different circles. We didn't socialize in the same groups at all. Really the only way we met was through my cousin. I was always at my cousin's house and he was around. Eventually we started dating, nothing serious at first."

Debbie was 17 at the time and Johnny was 20, an age difference both families thought was too great. "Nobody wanted us to date," she says. But they didn't listen to anybody else. They dated for three years before they got engaged, but once engaged they wasted no time getting married.

"We had already planned it all out. I think we were only engaged for like six weeks before we got married."

The pair had already made several trips to the jeweler checking out rings, but when Debbie suggested they go look at a few more and make a decision, Johnny said no. It wasn't long before she realized why.

Johnny was working nights and called in sick so he could take Debbie out to dinner. But Johnny didn't just convince his boss he was sick, he went a little too far and Debbie thought he was sick, too.

"Let's go out to dinner," he said.

"You don't want to go out to dinner if you're sick," Debbie said, and was very reluctant to let up on the issue. She finally agreed to a small buffet where she knew Johnny could get some soup. "If you're sick you want soup, right?"

When they arrived at the restaurant, Johnny left the T-top of his Trans-Am open and didn't realize it until they got inside.

"We have got to sit by a window," he said.

"Why?"

"I need to be able to see the car."

"Nobody is going to steal your car. Quit worrying about it."

He worried all through dinner and Debbie was convinced he had gone completely whacko. Later in the evening she understood.

"When he proposed and gave me the ring, he told me that he had left it in the car. That is why he was insistent on keeping an eye on the car. I laughed." And she said yes. They married shortly after that, in August of 1986.

Johnny was already racing when they started to date, but it was more of a hobby. He was a tool and die maker and he raced dirt cars on the weekends. When he decided to take some time off from racing, everybody blamed the new girlfriend. But Johnny was simply trying to figure out if he wanted to keep racing, and if he did want to keep it up, he was pondering a switch to asphalt.

During this time, Debbie was getting her accounting degree from Grand Valley State University near Grand Rapids.

Johnny won a local championship in '89 and then took over Butch Miller's ride in ASA in 1990. "Once he started driving ASA, that is when he decided he wanted to be a driver. He said, 'I want to race Winston Cup.'"

Johnny's performance in ASA had caught the attention of some key players in the racing world, including the late Dale Earnhardt, who was considering putting Johnny in his Busch Series car. A sponsor conflict prevented that, but Earnhardt began a campaign to get Johnny a full-time ride. Earnhardt and Ernie Irvan began touting this kid they had seen running ASA.

"This new kid is the hottest thing since sliced bread," Irvan said. That was enough to convince car owner Bill Baumgardner. Baumgardner was set to have Johnny run for Busch Series Rookie of the Year in 1994, and although he was less than thrilled to discover this "kid" was 31 years old, the deal was done.

And that meant Johnny and Debbie had to move south.

At the time the decision didn't seem like a difficult one. Probably because it took Debbie several years to realize just what she had done.

"I never knew what I wanted to do, but when I went to college I just loved accounting. I got this job right away and I started at the bottom and I was working my way up and I loved it. I had a career going. Accounting was it. You either love it or you hate it, but to me it makes perfect sense. It is so logical and there are rules and you follow the rules. I guess that is how my mind works."

Her boss was appalled that she would quit at age 29, on her way up the corporate ladder.

"But I didn't hesitate. John had this opportunity to race Busch cars so we were going, no matter what. But I never realized I was giving up my whole career. I was kind of burned out at the time; I think that is why it didn't really hit me. I just thought maybe I'll take this summer off and go to the races and stuff and I'll look for a job in the fall."

It just hadn't occurred to her how different the Busch Series would be from ASA. During Johnny's rookie year in 1994, the schedule covered twenty-six weekends across fifteen states. These were not one-day

shows, but usually two, or sometimes three. But none of that had figured into the equation when Debbie encouraged Johnny to take the chance. To her it was only logical—her husband wanted to drive stock cars at the Winston Cup level. "You do what you have to do."

Johnny's family wasn't happy with the idea of them up and moving to North Carolina. They encouraged them to just try it for a little while and see if it worked out. Debbie said no. "If you want to be a race car driver, we're selling the house and we're moving down there. If this team doesn't work out, we've got to stay down there and find another one. So let's go.

"John was probably pretty relieved that I had that attitude. I had no idea what to expect. But we were young enough not to put too much thought into it. We didn't have any kids and if it didn't work out, we could go home with our tails between our legs and start over. There are few opportunities like that in life."

Johnny made the move pay off quickly by claiming Rookie of the Year honors in '94, with nine top-10 and six top-5 finishes, including his first career Busch Series win at Dover Downs. Johnny backed that up by becoming the first Busch Series driver to win the championship one year after claiming rookie honors. He won two races in 1995—Atlanta Motor Speedway and Hickory Motor Speedway—and secured the championship with nineteen top-10 and twelve top-5 finishes.

Meanwhile Debbie was discovering that Southerners viewed racing in a whole different light than did people in Michigan.

"When we lived in Michigan and people would ask, 'What does your husband do?' I would say he's a race car driver, and they would be like, 'Oh, really,' almost with a tone of sympathy or disdain. Down here they want to know who his sponsor is, what's his car number. They are all into it. It is more accepted as a legitimate profession here."

Maintaining the idea that the first season in North Carolina was just a summer off, Debbie casually perused the Charlotte paper for jobs. "John would laugh at me because I would find something and say, 'Oh, here's the perfect job for me. Where's Asheville?'" Asheville is about 150 miles from Charlotte.

Eventually the reality crept in. "This is a business. This is everyone's full-time job, whereas in ASA at that time, some of the drivers still had regular jobs and the crew members had regular jobs and just raced on the weekends."

It meant that racing was going to have to become her full-time occupation as well.

"When I left Michigan, I didn't realize that I was giving up anything. I really thought I was taking a month, maybe the summer off. But after that first summer of racing, I realized the commitment involved with the sport. If I wanted my marriage to work, I had to give up the idea of any sort of career. I knew there was no way to have both. I was going to have to travel to keep my family and marriage together.

"It isn't just the job that I gave up. I gave up my life. I don't think any of the men realize what the women give up to be with them. Racing consumes your entire family. I think every wife in this sport has been at a crossroads at some point with the intensity involved with this business. You make a choice and find ways to make peace with it. The result is worth it: You get precious time with your husband and family.

"I really had no clue what we were getting into. That's why we moved without giving it a second thought, because I had no clue about the schedule and everything that was involved with this business."

Outside of racing, most people work Monday through Friday. Then on weekends, especially during the spring and summer, they spend time with their neighbors cooking out, or chatting by the back fence instead of actually mowing the lawn. They go to a neighborhood church on Sunday mornings.

"You don't get to know your neighbors at home and you don't have that church base because you are always gone," Debbie says.

"It was during John's first year of Winston Cup [1996] that he said, 'Let's get a motor home.' I was pregnant with Katelyn at the time and I just didn't want to spend money that we didn't have. But a week or so after she was born, we ordered one. I hadn't been

able to go to any of the races that year and he really wanted me there.

"So with the motor home, that area becomes your neighborhood family. All the kids play together. You'll see a lot of people do their birthday parties at the [Motor Racing Outreach community center because that is where you're among family and friends. I don't think any other sport is like that."

Katelyn, born in March '96, and Mikayla, born in November '97, like many other racing kids, have been raised in a motor home, so it is only logical that they assume everyone has one of those traveling havens.

"It's hard because the other day I was taking some clothes to Goodwill and Katelyn asked why we were giving our clothes away.

"They don't fit anymore and this organization will give them to people who can't afford to buy new clothes," Debbie explained.

"That's good. But if somebody doesn't have a house to live in, they just live in their motor home, right?"

Debbie tried to explain to her daughter that she and her sister were very lucky to have a motor home and be able to travel with their dad like they do. "If I do my job right they will grow up understanding how lucky they are and that their life is not the norm."

The growth of the traveling community center has had a tremendous impact on today's racing family. With the schedule growing every year—up to 36 points races and 38 weekends in 2001—MRO and the community center provide a place for the families to relax, be together, and retreat from the chaos of the garage area.

"It's just unbelievable the changes I've seen in just the five years that we've been in Winston Cup, with MRO and the inclusion of the family. When you have kids everything changes and you don't want anything infringing on your private time. You have so little of it. MRO has been huge. It gives [the kids] something to do. It's a good base because, traveling all the time, you don't get to live your church life at home and that has always been very important to me."

Needless to say, the girls keep both Debbie and Johnny grounded in an otherwise chaotic atmosphere.

When it came time to come up with names for them, like many parents, Debbie wanted to be unique. So, she thought a simple spelling quirk would be enough. She chose to spell Katelyn that way. She never saw it spelled like that before. "Now everybody in Michigan spells it that way."

The name Mikayla came about a bit differently.

"The second year the teams raced in Japan, I flew to Hawaii. John raced and then flew to Hawaii and met me on his way back. I got to the hotel about 12 or so hours before John did, and everywhere I went in the hotel that day, I would run into this little girl named Mikayla. One day all three of us were in the elevator together and after she got off I told John that was Mikayla. 'She's been following me.' He said he liked that name, so when I got pregnant again and said, 'Let's talk about baby names,' he said, 'We already have the name.'

"What do you mean?"

"Well, we didn't use the boy name before and if we have another girl we are going to use that macadamia name."

"You like the name but you can't remember it."

Then Johnny promised that if they named a girl Mikayla, he would remember it and not call her "macadamia."

Having children tends to alter every parent's perspective on life and priorities. The Bensons are no different. So how does a mother deal with the prospect that the job her husband does could end his life at any given moment?

"I don't let myself think about it. He is following his dream. I don't think about the

• • •

danger factor. You can't think about it too much or you will go crazy.

"Whenever he has a bad wreck, I'll say, 'Why is it that you want to do this?' But I have got myself so conditioned [to understand] that these drivers are as safe as can be. Look at the wrecks we have seen and they walk away. I think one other good thing is that the wrecks I call his two really bad ones, I didn't see happen."

The first of these bad wrecks was at Michigan in the 1994 Busch race.

Johnny was on the back stretch when the spotter came across the radio and said, "He got hit … he's in the air … he's flipping."

Debbie and the crew chief looked at each other. "Who is he talking about?"

"Johnny just flipped."

"How bad is the car, are we still in the race?" was the question from Debbie, not the crew chief. She was quickly informed that Johnny's car had flipped over.

"You mean like in the air?" She had no concept that cars flipped over. "ASA cars don't do that, so I didn't think about that happening." They never heard anything from Johnny over the radio, but between the spotter and television, and radio broadcasts, they found out he was out of the car and walking and talking.

"I went to the care center and I wasn't really concerned. I still had not seen the replay yet. So we were in the hotel later that night and saw one angle of the wreck and I thought, 'Well, that didn't look that bad.' Then they showed another and we both said, 'Oh yeah, that looked pretty bad.' But once you know they are out of the car and walking and talking, all the fear goes away."

The second big wreck was at Charlotte during Johnny's rookie year in Winston Cup. Debbie had just had Katelyn two months before. Katelyn had diaper rash and was uncomfortable at the racetrack. Their motor home hadn't arrived yet, so Debbie decided to leave the track early and get Katelyn home where she would feel better.

"I was actually on my way to the car when the wreck happened." Johnny and Ricky Craven collided between turns 1 and 2, and Johnny's car virtually disintegrated. "I had my radio with me, but a friend had seen me and offered to take me out to my car on his

golf cart, so I'd turned my radio off and we were talking. When I got to my car and turned the radio on, they were headed into commercials and were saying, 'We'll tell you about the Benson-Craven wreck when we return.'

"My first thought was, 'Oh gosh, John blew a tire.' So I went back into the track and was waiting at the infield care center and everyone is panicking and wondering why I was so calm. I still had not seen what happened and I hadn't seen the car. I just knew he was out of the car and talking, so I didn't figure there was anything to be worried about.

"It was sort of funny later though; he bit his tongue during the wreck and he couldn't eat for a while, so I told everyone he was on a crash diet."

In the years since Debbie and Johnny moved, they have seen first-hand just about every test and challenge racing can offer, from a Busch Series championship to Winston Cup Rookie-of-the-Year honors. There was also the move at the end of the 1999 season from Roush Racing to an unsponsored car at Tyler Jet Motorsports. Lycos was secured as a sponsor on the eve of the 2000 Daytona 500, which Benson came within three laps of winning before Dale Jarrett was able to nose his car under Benson en route to victory. But halfway through the season, the team was in financial jeopardy and literally days from closing the doors, when MB2 Motorsports—now MBV—and Valvoline stepped in and bought the team.

Knowing what she knows now, would that decision to pack up and leave Michigan still be as easy?

"I'd do it again, definitely.

"We're following a dream."

Left: Johnny and Debbie in New York City at the Winston Cup Awards banquet. (Steven Rose/MMP, Inc.)

CAT
Racing

CHAPTER 3

GAIL DAVIS

The sign at the entrance to the complex may say Bill Davis Racing, but in conversation you almost never hear their names spoken separately.

"We are always Bill and Gail Davis. It's not Bill Davis or Gail Davis, always Bill and Gail," Gail says as she strolls through their racing facility in High Point, North Carolina. "I'm proud of that. We truly did and still do all of this together."

She proudly strolls through the 125,000-square-foot complex of race shop, offices, meeting rooms, showrooms, and machine shops as if it is her home.

When they began their business she kept the books, answered the phones, took care of payroll, basically did anything that didn't involve putting the car together. Now that they have a staff, Gail takes on more of an overseer role. She personally does the annual financial reports for the racing business, as well as for Bill Davis Trucking and the farm in Arkansas.

"As the race business got bigger and bigger, we have people to do those things and I am thrilled, because I can't travel like we do and take care of any of those things anymore," Gail says. "I don't really have a specific job description anymore."

As the self-described "keeper of the stuff," Gail has had autograph cards—from every driver and every car she and Bill have ever been associated with—framed and hung on the walls of either the Winston Cup or the Busch shop. She proudly points out the record number of single-season Busch Series pole awards (eleven) won in 1992 by that open-wheel kid they took a chance on, Jeff Gordon. They were able to keep and display the car Ward Burton guided to both the Davis' and Burton's first Winston Cup triumph at Rockingham in October 1995.

"We couldn't afford to keep any of the cars Mark [Martin] and Jeff [Gordon] won

Opposite: Bill and Gail stand proudly in their High Point, North Carolina shop. The operation has grown from one small 10,000-square-foot building to several covering more than 125,000 square feet. (Gail Davis collection)

with because we needed the money then," Gail laments, as she thinks back to those days in the late '80s and early '90s. "Those were raced again or sold to other teams.

"This [2002] was our 16th season in racing. I have a photo album of every year we have raced. If somebody comes in and wants to write a story or needs some background info, I have it all right here."

Those books are stored in massive storage cabinets that line the walls of her expansive office that she shares with their dog, Short Track—Short for short. As we're talking, Short lifts his head wearily, but offers only a few wags of his tail, unconcerned about any visitors who might follow Gail into the office, just very content that she has returned.

"I was working out earlier in our workout room and Short, I guess, woke up and got to worrying about me. He came to the double doors that lead to the shop and just started barking until he saw me." That was all he needed. Secure in the knowledge that she was still in the building, Short returned to his bed in her office.

"He is his own celebrity. He has his own fans who come by and ask for him and bring him milk bones, and he loves to go over to MRO to see the kids. He will even fly with the crew when Bill and I are riding our motorcycles, and the guys will bring him to meet us at the track."

As Gail sits behind her desk where her 2002 Daytona 500 champion ring is displayed proudly in a glass and wooden case, she still has a hard time believing how far they have come.

"We weren't wealthy people to start off with, but we used our money wisely. We put the money back into the company. We are in debt to our real estate, but that is it. Whatever the business needs, we get. That is how we have been successful. We didn't do much for ourselves away from the business."

All of it is such a far cry from the early days of their marriage when Bill lived in a motor home behind the 10,000-square-foot race shop in High Point, while Gail was nearly 1,000 miles away in Arkansas, running Bill Davis Trucking.

The pair met when Gail ran a bottled-water distributing company in central Arkansas. She made a sales call to the Peterbuilt truck company in Little Rock where Bill worked, and since she was short a deliveryman, Bill assisted her in lugging the clumsy 60-pound bottle of water into the office. A communication between the two began when Gail hired a friend of Bill's to fill that empty deliveryman slot.

"Bill started coming over and calling and stuff. Before you knew it, we were involved." Her life to that point had been largely unsettled as Gail herself tried to find a direction.

Gail was the last of four children, born "just when my mother was sure she wasn't having any more children. My mother and my oldest sister had babies five weeks apart. My sister was 18 and my mother was 36."

After growing up in Batesville, Arkansas, Gail went to college simply because she just knew she should go, but she lacked direction and left after one year. She headed to Little Rock, and then farther west to Albuquerque, New Mexico, and then Los Angeles. "When you grow up in a small town you don't want to stay in that small town," Gail says. She married an engineer she met in California. That marriage lasted six years, but the divorce took its toll.

"I felt terribly guilty for years and years and years over getting a divorce. Nobody in my family had ever gotten one. People just didn't get divorced. That was a trying time.

"I still maintain a relationship with his son that he had from a previous marriage. That was important to me."

It was during that time that she made her way back to Arkansas and found Bill. About a year after they met, Bill moved to Batesville, Arkansas to work for Julian Martin, Mark's late father, to learn how to run a trucking business. Bill wanted to own his own trucks.

"When I met Bill I recognized in him an ambition that I admired," Gail says. "Bill had a plan to make things happen. That is always what I lacked. I knew how to work hard, I just never knew what I wanted to do."

Bill and Gail have worked side-by-side—often literally, as Gail didn't have a separate

CAT
Racing

• • •

office until 1996. "My desk was always about five feet from Bill's" for the bulk of their 28-year relationship.

Bill had been exposed to racing while working with Julian. As so often happens, his involvement began as a small venture, a hobby, helping someone else.

As Bill spent more and more time racing and helping Julian get Mark's career going, Gail was left to hold up a very young trucking company. It was more than she could do. The couple had been married for just three years and Gail was overwhelmed. "Before we both moved to North Carolina I ran the trucking company and Bill went racing."

"It took me so long to get up the nerve to tell him that. I finally said, 'I can't do this anymore.' That was in 1984 and the company was young. I was doing everything while Bill was gone and the only other employees were a couple of mechanics. I'm one of those people that has a hard time saying 'no.' I always say, 'I'll do that.' So I was so afraid Bill wouldn't like me anymore if I couldn't do all of this stuff."

While Bill hardly abandoned the racing scene, he did put his hand back into the trucking business more to help Gail. But then it was Mark again who called Bill about getting into Busch Series racing.

"Somebody had asked Mark if he knew of anybody who would run him in the Busch Series on a limited schedule in 1989. We ran sixteen to eighteen races that first year of Busch out of Arkansas. There was a lot of travel, but I ran the trucking company, so I couldn't be gone. In 1990 Bill started talking about buying a shop in North Carolina. I thought 'My God, this is the end of everything. My husband's going to move half a continent away and leave me running this dang trucking company.'"

Bill moved to North Carolina and Gail stayed behind to keep the trucking company going, and the pair made it work until she too made the move to North Carolina.

"In 1993, we bought the house we still live in here. I'm proud of the fact that our businesses have always come first, whether it be the racing or the trucks, which is why we have a really nice place of business and it has taken me ten years to furnish my house here," she laughs. "We bought the house here and there was not a thing in it. I was not about to mess up my house in Arkansas. Not that I had anything to speak of anyway, I just wasn't ready to tear apart the house I considered our home.

Opposite: Gail and Bill share a kiss before a race in Fontana, California in the spring of 2000. (Gail Davis collection)

"So here we were in this 3,500-square-foot house with nothing in it and we go furniture shopping and what do we buy? A dining table!"

The High Point house is modest by the standards of most in the racing business, 3,500 square feet on an average-sized lot, and while they have added more furniture they still pour most of their money back into the businesses. But there is one love that success has afforded them to pursue—riding motorcycles.

"One of the greatest accomplishments of my life is learning to ride a motorcycle at age 50," says Gail.

Today Gail, 57, readily admits that if she could just ride motorcycles all the time she would be happy. "It is just wonderful."

But Gail's relationship with motorcycles was hardly love at first sight.

"Bill has had a motorcycle most of his life and I had ridden behind him twice and I was terrified … totally uninterested," Gail says.

When Kyle Petty came up with the idea of hosting a ride across the country for charity, the Make-A-Wish Foundation, Bill was one of the first in line to make that inaugural trip in 1995. Kyle's wife, Pattie, encouraged Gail to tag along, because Pattie was afraid there wouldn't be any other women on the trip.

"I said OK, but told her that I was riding in the motor coach. I'm not riding on one of those motorcycles," Gail says. MBNA was the Davis' sponsor at the time and provided a motor coach to accompany the Kyle Petty Charity Ride. "It was cold and they were going way too fast. So I was quite happy in the motor coach."

The ride traveled from San Jose, California, to Newport Beach on a dreary day one, and then the riders awoke to beautiful southern California sunshine. Gail had noticed there were several women on the ride. Pattie was riding behind Kyle and there were three women on their own bikes. So she decided to go ahead and ride behind Bill for a while.

"I rode the whole rest of the ride and I had a ball!"

She soon learned that one of the women on the ride had just ridden 60 miles by herself prior to riding across the country. "I said, you know, I think I could ride a motorcycle."

Bill responded by presenting Gail with a brand new BMW motorcycle on her 50th birthday in the fall of 1995.

"Well, I was very intimidated. Here was this enormous bike. I couldn't begin to hold it up."

She began what became an arduous process of learning to ride by borrowing a very small 80cc dirt bike and riding it around the back yard and through the neighborhood. Bill taught her the basics of shifting. Then when they went to Daytona in February for

Speedweeks, she enrolled in a three-day Motorcycle Safety Foundation course, in which students learn to ride a 250 Honda.

"I couldn't ride it, either," she says, still feeling the exasperation of years ago. "There was a woman instructor on a BMW, and there was an older male biker instructor and that man was sure that I would never be able to ride a motorcycle and was very, very critical of me and I was awful. I was scared. I tried to do what they said, and the woman was patient with me and I got through it."

But there was still the matter of the enormous BMW waiting for her at home. And the next Kyle Petty Charity Ride was just two months away.

"The minute I got on the BMW I fell right over! I think that first day I dropped it three times and Bill was ready to kill me."

Bill maintained his composure and they rode 60 miles that first day. Although she rode another 60 the very next day, when it was time to embark on the Kyle Petty Charity Ride, Gail got nervous.

"I was terrified. I knew I didn't have enough experience. Bill told me I'd be fine, but he always thinks that I can do anything. I rode 1,000 miles that day."

Gail also spent that night praying to God to make her sick so that she didn't have to ride the next day. "I was just so scared. It had been such a long, tiring day. But when I woke up I was fine, and I finished the ride. Now I've ridden about 43,000 miles on that BMW."

That includes one terrifying wreck en route to Pocono in July of 2001.

"One of the greatest thrills of riding a BMW motorcycle is riding curves," Gail says. "We rode the Blue Ridge Parkway all day, and of course, that's total curves. We had a wonderful time. Bill was on a new bike and a friend of ours was with us and we were taking our time.

"There had been a couple of really horrific rainstorms that we hadn't been in, but we had slowed and stopped a couple of times to let them pass. I was getting tired and it was getting late. We were already going to be way after dark getting to Pocono, so I told Bill we should head over to the interstate."

Gail let Bill and their friend go on ahead. "I had been keeping up all day, but it was starting to rain again and I just slowed up a bit, but I wasn't bothered by them being so far ahead."

As she entered the interstate outside of Luray, Virginia, Gail went into a big sweeping curve. "I didn't realize that I did anything wrong, but I felt the back get a little loose. I kind of thought I had it straightened up and then just as suddenly it was out from under me and I was sliding across the highway. I noticed there was a semi truck and there was other traffic, but it all happened so fast. I remember going across the highway and into the ditch in the opposite lane. When I quit rolling I remember thinking, 'I'm alive. I think I'm hurt, but I'm alive.'"

People surrounded her almost immediately, and fortunately, one of the cars that stopped had a doctor and a nurse inside. Bill had lost sight of Gail before the accident, but didn't wait very long to pull over when she hadn't come back into view.

"They were keeping me in sight in the rearview mirror and they rode slowly for me to catch up. When I didn't catch right up, they pulled over and Bill noticed the traffic backing up in the other direction, so he knew something had happened.

"He came roaring up and he kept saying, 'I'm sorry,' 'I'm sorry.' He felt like he had been going too fast and therefore I was going faster than I wanted to be. I guess I was, but I hadn't felt out of control."

A trip to the hospital revealed no major injuries, but she was severely bruised and she had hit her head. Without a helmet, the head injury would have been much more severe.

"I can somewhat identify with these drivers now when they hit their heads, because for the first two or three weeks I didn't feel quite like me. It was quite a while before I felt like I had my wits about me again."

Despite the pain and fear, Gail got right back on her bike as soon as it was repaired, and made the ride from Miami to Atlanta that fall.

"I was nervous and it rained on that trip, so that made me nervous. I am a little more

apprehensive about curves now. I don't know that I did anything wrong to cause my accident, but Bill likes to say, 'You ran out of talent, is what you did.' Which I guess I did at
that moment. That first ride back we rode very slowly and Bill was very patient, because
I am sure there are a lot of people who would never have gotten back on a bike again.
But I couldn't imagine that. It is truly one of my joys in life."

One of the Davis' other joys has become their ranch in Batesville. They were not
really thinking about buying anything at that time, much less a ranch, but another one of
those phone calls from Mark Martin changed their lives.

Mark's father, Julian, was killed in a plane crash in August 1998. Julian and his wife,
Shelly, had a large farm in Batesville with a new home on it that they had never lived in.
Mark wanted the Davises to buy it.

"The family would really like it if you all would buy the place," Mark said.

At Thanksgiving 1998, Bill and Gail decided to go look at the property before traveling to New York for the Winston Cup banquet, where they would then see Mark. They
assumed that they would tell him 'no.'

Once they saw it, the answer changed.

"It is an incredible, incredible place. I told Bill, 'If we do not buy this place we will
hate ourselves forever.'"

They did buy it, and had plans that, in the future, they would operate it as a working
cattle ranch. But the future came pretty quickly.

"We moved in March, and within thirty days we had some cows," Gail says. "We had
nine in that first batch. Now there are about 500."

Although Gail knows you aren't ever supposed to get attached, the cows' names are
based on who drives the car that matches their tag number. "They all have personalities
and you just can't help but get attached to them. It is a lot of fun. When we are there, I
love to go out in the mornings and evenings and help Bill feed. I really enjoy it."

Gail finds peace and fun in the cattle and the motorcycles. Although admittedly she
and Bill would like to have even more success in racing, they seem to be well past the
days when Gail looked at Bill and each one wondered if they shouldn't just go back to
Arkansas and the trucks.

"We are really happy with our life and our business. Bill talks about retiring sometimes, and that is what the cows are for, but every time he talks about it, it seems to
become more distant in the future. And that's fine, too. I'm not sure either one of us
knows how not to work."

NATIONAL TRAINING CENTER
STIHL
Coca-Cola
DODGE
Valvoline
Winston Cup Series
STIHL
DODGE
Coca-Cola

DANIELLE FRYE

CHAPTER 4

Danielle Fields was a Darrell Waltrip fan through and through.

The Pell City, Alabama, native lived just fifteen minutes from Talladega Superspeedway and frequently tagged along to the track on race weekends with her father, Lawrence.

Lawrence was a member of the White Flag Club, a group of volunteers who were responsible for handling pre-race and many post-race activities during the 1970s and early '80s. One of the perks of being a member of the White Flag Club was meeting and spending time with the drivers. The demands on a driver's time weren't nearly what they are today, so it was not at all out of the ordinary for Lawrence to bring a driver home to have dinner with the family on race weekends.

One morning in April 1983, Lawrence told his daughter that he might, just might, be able to get Darrell Waltrip to come and have dinner with the family. He didn't promise results, but he did promise to try. Well, to 12-year-old Danielle that was as good as a done deal.

"I went off to school that morning thinking, 'This is going to be so great!'" Danielle says. So when Lawrence came home with someone other than Darrell Waltrip, there was no consoling her.

"I didn't get Darrell Waltrip," Lawrence said. "But I got this new, up-and-coming driver."

"By that time I was mad," Danielle says. "I wasn't at all interested in hearing about this new driver. But my dad was insistent."

"Everybody says he is going to be really good. His name is Bill Elliott," her dad pleaded.

Opposite: Danielle celebrates Bill Elliott's win at the 2002 Brickyard 400 in Indianapolis with Bill, his wife Cindy, and son Chase. (Danielle Frye collection)

Danielle joined her parents, two brothers, and grandmother for dinner, but at first refused to acknowledge Bill. "I walked in and I didn't speak to him. I was still mad. I wanted Darrell Waltrip and I got Bill Elliott. I was not happy," she laughs, openly acknowledging that she had been more than a bit rude.

By the end of the evening, her tune had changed dramatically, and the pair have been, as Danielle says, "fast friends ever since." Not to mention that Elliott has lifelong fans in Danielle and her family.

To that point, racing had just been something of a novelty in Danielle's life, certainly not a passion. It was impossible to grow up near Talladega and not pay at least some attention, plus her dad's volunteer job afforded her the privilege of attending the races and she became something of a fan.

"I was too young to get into the pits or the garage, but I was always the one on the fence," Danielle says. "I remember meeting Bobby and Davey Allison. They came over to me on my birthday and signed something for me, which even then was so cool."

But it was the night with Bill Elliott that altered the course of her life. "I knew from then on that I was somehow going to get involved in racing. It was really the people that I loved, especially if you connected with them somehow."

Danielle's career path was chosen and she would not waver.

After graduating from Pell City High School, she attended Troy State in south Alabama on a basketball scholarship. She earned her degree in broadcast journalism and public relations and wasted no time getting right to work after completing her courses in 1993.

"I had done my internship with *Racing for Kids* magazine and Griggs Publishing, so I was able to go right to work out of school as a staff writer and director of promotions."

Danielle had friends at the time who were eager to finish college not so they could go to work, but so they could take a break and travel. "Not me. I was ready to get going. I finished up my courses in the winter quarter and moved [to Charlotte] in March."

That driven nature has followed her throughout her career. She got her first taste of public relations with Creative Marketing Group, where her responsibilities included PR for Shawna Robinson in the Busch Series. That was the year that Shawna won the pole for the Busch race in Atlanta. From there Danielle went into the production side of television at World Sports.

One of the shows she worked on was Darrell Waltrip's. "I told

him the story about dinner and Bill Elliott and that I had been a huge fan of his. He thought it was funny, but when I left World Sports to go to work for Bill, Darrell asked, 'Did I do something wrong?'"

Danielle had been with World Sports for only about six months before she was offered the opportunity to work with Bill Elliott doing public relations for McDonalds and thus her close friend. Their relationship brought both advantages and disadvantages. First, Danielle knew Bill and his family very well and knew what kind of stories to pitch to the media. But the friendship didn't keep Bill from testing her and questioning many of the appearances and interviews she lined up for him.

"I told him that he didn't know how many times I said 'no,' so when I said 'yes' he had to trust me. If I screwed up and we did something that we probably shouldn't have, I'd admit it and we wouldn't do it again. But we had a great level of trust there on both sides."

It was also during this time that Danielle made another major change in her life.

Rick Humphrey had been working for Sports Marketing Enterprises, the outside marketing arm of RJ Reynolds. The nature of the racing circuit is that you have this traveling family that you see every weekend. The pair would see each other at the racetrack, and finally met officially at a party and "Things just kind of went from there." They married in 1995 and at the end of 1996, Rick was offered an opportunity to take over public relations at Talladega. It was a move that those on the outside looking in figured Danielle had pushed for.

Daily Home   Monday, January 9, 1989

Danielle Fields (with ball) and Larry Slater's Pell City Lady Panthers square off with another tough contender on Tuesday, as the Wenonah Lady Dragons come calling (BOB CRISP photo)

" 'I was so career focused, I wanted to do whatever I could to do the job well,' Danielle admits. 'Our jobs had flip-flopped. He had done all of his traveling and had gotten it out of his system. I was just getting started.' "

• • •

"That was just not the case," Danielle says. "I had very mixed emotions about that move. At that time, I was working for McDonalds out of my house. I was worried if we moved to Pell City, the job might go away. Then what? What if McDonalds doesn't agree to let me move down there? I really worried about all of this stuff. In the end they let me move and it was all OK. But the major downfall was the travel. To get to Birmingham you had to make four or five connections. I spent a lot of time in the Charlotte airport."

It was a transition point for both of their careers. Rick had been traveling every weekend for several years with SME. Now with the speedway, he wasn't traveling nearly as much—occasionally to other International Speedway Corporation–owned tracks, but even that wasn't often. By contrast, Danielle's career was growing in step with the sport, and when she began working for McDonalds and Bill, she was traveling more than ever.

"I was so career focused, I wanted to do whatever I could to do the job well," Danielle admits. "Our jobs had flip-flopped. He had done all of his traveling and had gotten it out of his system. I was just getting started.

"Even though I worked at home, it was full-bore work. He would come home at night and we would eat dinner and then I would go right back into my little office and work. I know that wasn't very smart on my part, but it was what was important to me then. There just wasn't any balance."

The marriage ended amicably five years later.

When McDonalds made the decision to step back and reevaluate its involvement in NASCAR, Danielle was offered a chance to work for another sponsor. Bill was not keen on losing the comfort level he had with Danielle for someone he didn't really know, but Danielle saw an opportunity she needed to take.

" 'You drove for your family for all those years and then you broke away to drive for Junior Johnson to see what was out there,'" she told Bill. "'Well, that's what I want to do.' It was tough, but we were friends before I worked with him and that wasn't going to change if I took a different job."

The job was with Ford and public relations for Dale Jarrett and Quality Care. She was there for just one year, but it was the right year. While the job was essentially the same as the one she did for Bill and McDonalds, there were differences.

Bill never won a race during Danielle's tenure, so when she was told where the victory lane hats were on the No. 88 truck, she says, "I was like, what do I do with those?"

Jarrett won four races en route to his Winston Cup Championship in 1999.

"It was great," Danielle says. "I've always been competitive. I was taught that nobody remembers second. For me to be able to be a part of a championship was great. I know I didn't have anything to do with the car or anything, but I was still a part of it. That year is something I will always have and I am so grateful that I got to experience that."

So what does one do after learning the ropes doing PR for a close friend, then working with a championship team? "How much higher can you go?" Danielle says. "The next logical step? You go to the sanctioning body."

Danielle began the new millennium as the communications director for NASCAR. "Team PR was a great fit for me because I was able to generate a lot of publicity, through my competitive nature, into pulling for, or I guess, 'selling' my team. Then transferring over to NASCAR, I had to pull for everybody. I wasn't really selling anymore. The other main difference was that now I had to keep up with everything, rules changes and violations that I had never thought about before unless they applied directly to my team. I had to have answers when crew chiefs had questions."

Danielle's new job involved being the liaison between the media and NASCAR, and handling announcements of rules changes as well as rules violations. Her position also put her on the front lines when tragedies occurred. She was the one in front of the cameras, explaining an always-difficult situation.

That first situation came in New Hampshire in the fall of 2000. Kenny Irwin was killed on the same track that had claimed Adam Petty's life in the spring of that year.

"When I got the word that it had been a fatal accident … I didn't have time to feel anything. You can't. Because you can't walk into a pressroom crying, you just can't. So I never let myself get emotional until I am by myself in my hotel room. You don't allow yourself to feel.

"You go in and you do what you have to do and then later you let go. You have to do that or you will explode."

"Crisis communications is something I had never really had a hand in before. There are people that think you should have all this training, and I do think you need to be prepared, but it is really difficult because you don't know how you are going to react until you are in the situation."

Below: Danielle shares a laugh with 2002 Winston Cup Champion Tony Stewart at the NASCAR Awards Banquet. (Steven Rose/MMP, Inc.)

Her experience caused her to urge other team PR reps to have a plan in place. "It doesn't only apply to the racetrack. We travel so much. There are things that can happen away from the track as well. You still never know how you will react, but you still need to try to be as prepared as you can be."

Danielle had become the consummate professional. She managed a championship tour of New York with Jarrett, and she appeared to make the transition to NASCAR seamlessly. But there was one situation she was always prepared for that she had not yet experienced.

A key element of her PR repertoire when she represented Bill Elliott, from 1995 to 1998, was the daunting fact that the last time Bill had won a race was the Southern 500 at Darlington in 1994. With each passing year, the media began to write off Bill more. He was getting older, he was no longer in a winning situation, and so on. Was the Ray Evernham/Bill Elliott Dodge team going to pay off with a win, or just a lot of publicity for Dodge?

"I never thought he couldn't win again. I always defended him. Somebody that has that much talent and skill doesn't just lose it."

So when Bill finally won in Homestead in the 2001 season, Danielle headed straight to victory lane. There were comments here and there from members of the media about her favoring Bill, but not from the people who mattered. "It was an unwritten rule that I wanted to see Bill do well, and when he did I was going to congratulate him.

"It was great. I was there with them in victory lane at the Brickyard, too. These are my friends. Bill is like family. I am just so happy to see him doing what he is capable of doing again."

With new racetracks popping up all across the country and more and more teams to keep track of, NASCAR expanded its Daytona Beach–based offices to North Carolina, where most of the teams are based. In September of 2001, Danielle was given the go-ahead to move to Charlotte. It made sense to have the communications director in close proximity to the teams.

Danielle continued to focus all of her energy on her career. A new relationship just wasn't on her mind, but that didn't keep her good friend Karen Byrnes from trying to matchmake. Karen kept mentioning Jay Frye, general manager at MBV/MB2 Motorsports, which fields the No. 10 car driven by Johnny Benson and the No. 01 driven by Jerry Nadeau. Danielle knew who he was, just as she knew everyone at the track that she saw frequently, but she didn't know him well. For more than a year, she discouraged Karen from setting up a date.

"Jay found me," Danielle says. "I kept putting Karen off and it was never anything against him, I just wasn't interested in anyone, or in being fixed up."

Danielle had already planned to take the weekend of September 14 off and was planning to visit Charlotte to look at houses. She had spoken to Jay at the annual Labor Day race in Darlington a couple of weeks before and told him that she would be in Charlotte that weekend. When the September 11 tragedy happened, everyone in racing spent the following weekend at home. Danielle still made the trip to Charlotte and when Jay asked her to dinner, she finally said sure.

"We've been together ever since. That is what makes me so mad. It was instant and I wasted all this time telling Karen 'no' and I could have been with him. After our first date I said to myself I am probably going to marry this man, I love him so much.

I used to read things in Cosmo about these kinds of romances and I thought, 'Give me a break, these people are so creative in their writing.'

"We went out on September 15 and we married May 10. People say that we rushed into it. I say, 'If you know, you know.'" They married in St. Thomas and their families met for the first time on the flight to the island. "It was so cool. Everybody had such a great time."

Danielle remains very close to her family. Her mom, Brenda, usually joins Danielle on race day at Talladega, since that is one of the few times the hectic schedule affords her some time with her daughter.

Brenda has also become more of a race fan than she was before. She keeps up with the race on Sunday and is well aware of who's who when she attends the races with Danielle. "She had already met Jeff Gordon and Dale Jarrett, but this day she wanted to have her picture taken with Dale Jr.," Danielle says of a spring race in 2001. She made arrangements with Jr.'s PR rep, and after driver introductions, Danielle introduced Jr. to her mom. He gave her a big hug and posed for a photo before hopping on a golf cart to head to his car.

Unbeknownst to Danielle or her mother, a local film crew was nearby filming footage to use as promotional material for the fall race. As fall rolled around, people started seeing footage of Brenda being hugged by Dale Jr., with the words "…women are paying to be hugged by Dale Jr."

"Needless to say, she was pretty mortified. Now when she goes to the track she'll shake their hands, but one time I remember Bobby Labonte put his arm around her and she looked around for cameras."

You would think that Danielle's two brothers, Scott and Blair, would frequently be in line to grab those hard-to-get tickets and pit passes, but that has happened only once. "I have always been a huge Dan Marino fan," Danielle says. "So has my younger brother Blair, so in 1997 when Dan Marino came to the Pepsi 400 race, my brother came to meet Dan and then went back to the hotel to watch the race."

Ranking right up there with meeting Dan Marino was her 2001 meeting with President George W. Bush. "Dale Jarrett was in Washington, D.C. doing something for Ford. Mike Helton and Kevin Triplett had a meeting, so I thought since everyone was going to be there I would put together a media lunch. I really wanted to find a way to go along."

Unbeknownst to Danielle, her media lunch was about to take a back seat to a more important person.

"We were in this restaurant and this guy that we knew from the White House comes up and says, 'Mike, I hate to interrupt, but Mr. President can meet with you in 15 minutes.' We were hurried down the block and into the White House and there stands Condoleezza Rice. The next thing you know we hear, 'Big Mike, how are you?' And that was the president calling Mike, 'Big Mike.' Kevin and I just kind of looked at each other in disbelief."

Barely into her 30s, Danielle has already put together a very accomplished résumé in racing, but as the 2003 season began she was adding yet another job title to the list—Motor Racing Network (MRN) pit reporter.

She has a degree in broadcast journalism, and in 1999, before she began working for NASCAR, Danielle had worked the pits for a couple of Busch Series races. When she took the job with NASCAR, any work with MRN became a conflict of interest. But Danielle had really enjoyed the work. When Jim Phillips retired at the end of last season, MRN contacted Danielle.

"The timing was right," Danielle says. "I wasn't looking to leave NASCAR, but I was thinking of finding another job to do in NASCAR when [MRN executive producer] David Hyatt called."

So Danielle resigned from NASCAR. Her duties for MRN began during Speedweeks 2003; she has the unenviable task of interviewing the drivers after they exit the infield care center or after they have found themselves back in the garage early. "They are always really delightful then," she laughs. Even as she patrols pit road and the garage, rain-soaked and a bit frustrated during the lengthy rain delays that plagued the 2003 Daytona 500, she manages a smile, says with genuine enthusiasm, "I'm having a blast."

DARLINGTON
too tough to tame

LESA FRANCE KENNEDY

CHAPTER 5

The drivers' meeting is less than an hour away.

Mariah Carey is preparing to sing the national anthem. John Travolta is on hand to give the start command. Evander Holyfield is out and about shaking hands. The spectacle that is the 2003 Daytona 500 is nearing the drop of the green flag.

With just hours to go, one of the key players in making this all happen sits calmly in a motor home just a few yards from the entrance to the garage. She watches the flurry of activity outside the door, glances at her son playing a video game, and sips her coffee, as if the exterior chaos is soothing to her.

In a way, it should be. Daytona International Speedway is Lesa France Kennedy's second home. "My brother and I would come out here and sometimes we would ride our bikes around the track," she says. "I learned to drive a car out here. My dad decided it was the best place to learn to drive a car because I couldn't hit anybody," she laughs as she reminisces. She can still see that young girl, with Bill France Jr. teaching her to drive.

That girl is now 41 with an 11-year-old son, and is the newly named president of International Speedway Corporation, which owns thirteen tracks including California, Chicagoland, Darlington, Daytona, Kansas, Richmond, and Talladega. "The official announcement is a few months away, if I don't screw up too bad between now and then," Lesa laughs.

Lesa didn't get where she is by screwing up. Although being the daughter of Bill France Jr. ensured she would learn the business, it didn't guarantee that she would learn well. She did that on her own.

Lesa began her career in the ticket office as a teenager before going off to Duke University, where she graduated in 1983 with a degree in economics and psychology.

Opposite: Lesa and her father Bill France Jr. (Lesa Kennedy collection)

going on medically. I think having that knowledge is just so helpful. If I had been without some knowledge of what was happening, it would have been a lot more difficult."

"All signs right now are that Dad is in charge," she says proudly.

Lesa doesn't have a favorite driver, although she says everybody was a Richard Petty fan when she was growing up. As she says that, Ben, 11, walks through the room and adjusts his Jeff Gordon hat. "He has been a Jeff fan since he was five. That's his deal and he doesn't waver at all." But when it comes to his future, Ben doesn't have his sights set on being a driver. "Ben wants to be Mr. France," Lesa says.

Lesa's one long-term goal is to have the business go to the fourth generation of France children. "I base my decisions on that. That has me looking at things more for the long run than the short run. I think it would be neat to have the business go to the fourth generation and stay in the family forever."

Below: Lesa and Ben spend as much time together as they can doing outdoor activities. Ben does enjoy racing and has been a Jeff Gordon fan for years, but he doesn't want to be a driver—he wants to be Bill France. (Lesa Kennedy collection)

Opposite: Bruce, Lesa, Betty Jane, and Brian. (Lesa Kennedy collection)

KATIE KENSETH

Katie Martin smiled and glanced downward, unable to hide the blush on her cheeks. She was suddenly the center of attention, something that made her very uneasy.

"It's beautiful," someone cooed.

"Thank you," Katie said, with a look at the engagement ring on her finger.

"Was it romantic?" "What did he say?" The inquiries were being fired away from these well-meaning friends, many of whom she had met only recently. Katie was still adjusting to the fact that her recent engagement was of interest to more than just her family and friends and those of her fiancé, Winston Cup driver Matt Kenseth.

"He just very nicely asked," she responded, as she once again stole a glimpse at the sparkling diamond Matt had given her just a week ago, seemingly at times unsure if it was truly on her finger. Dressed in overalls and a T-shirt, Katie was trying to treat this day as just another Wednesday in January 2000. Just another ladies' Bible Club meeting—a group organized by Jackie Pegram and Motor Racing Outreach for women involved with men in racing. The group offers the ladies a chance to study the Bible, but maybe even more important, a chance to commune with other women who understand what it means to be married to men whose religion is racing.

Katie was among friends, albeit relatively new ones, and this shy farm girl, not yet 21 years old, was still learning about racing and the popularity that surrounded it. She could deal with the questions from friends and other wives who wanted to check out her diamond. That she understood.

But there was little anyone could do to prepare the very private Katie for the spotlight that was about to move its glare not only to her future husband, but also to her and her life away from the racetrack.

Opposite: Katie knew nothing about racing when she met Matt Kenseth and it took some time for the very-private Katie to adjust. (Steven Rose/MMP, Inc.)

• • •

Matt was about to begin his Winston Cup career, battling friend and Busch Series rival Dale Earnhardt Jr. for Rookie-of-the-Year honors. He was making the move up with his Busch series sponsor DeWalt, as well as his Busch Series crew under the guidance of Jack Roush and his mentor, Mark Martin. As if that wasn't enough to come to grips with, Matt started off the year 2000 by asking Katie to become his wife.

"We had been talking about it, but it was like, someday we'll do this, someday we'll do that. With everything Matt had going on with racing, I honestly didn't know when that day would be. I just knew we would be together and that was what mattered."

But she didn't expect her impending wedding would be splashed all over the Internet and the newspapers. "That's our private life. How we met and how he proposed, they don't need to know that. I think it's neat enough that they get to meet him at autograph sessions or in the garage. Stuff like that should be enough. I don't want to be rude to people or anything, but I guess I find it important to hang onto the private parts of our life.

"A lot of people ask me, 'What's it like to be Matt Kenseth's fiancée?' I say, 'Well, are you engaged or married? What's it like to be with your husband?' That is who he is to me. Obviously we do different things than a lot of people, but when you boil it down, it's the same. We are people too. People in love, planning a wedding. But the fans get excited and I heard one woman say once, 'Wow! I just talked to Matt Kenseth's fiancée.' That just floors me. I'm just Katie."

Just Katie. A young woman who grew up on a Wisconsin farm, who chose radiology as a major in college because it was on the page she randomly opened a college course book to, and who didn't have a hard time leaving that field of study after meeting Matt.

"I was filling out my forms for school. I opened the course book and it fell open to radiology and I thought, 'Well, this is interesting,' so that is what I put down for my major. That's horrible, isn't it? That really is all of the thought I put into it at the time."

When she told her parents, they told her she was crazy. "Katie, you do realize that means you will be working in a hospital?" her mom, Karen, said.

Hospitals and Katie have never mixed very well. When her younger brother was born, Katie passed out when she walked into the room. She went to visit her grandmother after

she had had knee surgery, and passed out. She knew all of this when she filled out the form, but her love of anatomy outweighed her fear of hospitals, and she thought it might be different if she were at the hospital studying. It wasn't.

"I hated it. I liked the classroom part of it. I love anatomy and learning about the body and bones and the way we are put together, but I would see the blood and the pain. I would actually pass out. I finally went to see my teacher, but she wouldn't let me quit because my grades were so good. I was on the dean's list. We agreed that I would finish that semester and take my anatomy credits and put them to use elsewhere. There was no way I could stay in radiology. If somebody needed me and I was passed out in the corner, what good was that going to do?"

Then in January 1999, Katie attended the wedding of her sister's brother-in-law, who happened to be a friend of Matt Kenseth's. Matt was in the wedding and it didn't take the two long to find each other. Small talk was made, phone numbers were exchanged, but racing was not discussed.

"I was clueless as to what he did, even after the first couple of times we went out. He was just a cute guy that I met at a wedding. He very rarely talked about racing and I knew nothing about it, so it didn't really register."

Eventually Katie started watching Matt race. At that time he was challenging Dale Earnhardt Jr. for the Busch Series title.

"He won the first race I ever went to [the Darlington Busch race in March 1999], but what I remember the most is

Visine
THE RED OUT®
Valvoline
Matt Kenseth
NAPA AUTO PARTS 300
76
2-19-00

driving back to the hotel after [the final practice session] and he said that was the worst car he had ever driven: 'The thing was a piece of junk.' Yet he won the race the next day, so I didn't understand that at all.

"Of course, I thought they just unloaded the cars, drove a couple of laps, and then lined them up to race. I didn't realize there was so much changing and fine tuning."

The girls back at school in Madison thought she was nuts. Here was this guy who lived all the way down in North Carolina. Her whole family, her whole life was in Wisconsin. He raced cars. She knew nothing about racing. None of that changed the fact that Katie had met 'the one.'

"I thought about Matt all the time. You know when you look at someone and you get that feeling in your stomach? It never went away for me."

Not only that, the phone bills were getting way out of hand. "I don't even know what we talked about, just normal, simple stuff. We would talk about each other's day. I used to dread the phone bill. It was always the running joke with my roommates to see how much it was going to be. My 'half' was always more like three-fourths of the total."

Discussions had begun in very general terms about Katie moving to North Carolina, but no date or even time frame had been determined. She was still so young, just 20, and very attached to her family. But she also knew she was in love with Matt and that was going to require her to make the move.

Matt called the Monday before the Busch race at Indianapolis Raceway Park in August 1999.

"Were you serious when you said you would move down here?" Matt asked.

"Yeah, I was."

"Well, how about Friday? You can put all your stuff in your car and follow my dad to Indy, then I'll drive with you to North Carolina."

This was it. The decision wasn't the hard part. Katie was at her parents' house and spent an hour sitting on the edge of the bed in her room staring at the wall. "How am I going to get up the courage to go downstairs and break it to my mom and dad that I am going to move to North Carolina, on Friday?"

She crept downstairs, sat at the table with her dad, and tentatively asked him if he thought her car would make it to North Carolina. The implication was not lost on him.

"Are you sure this is what you want?" he asked.

"Yes."

The next morning she awoke to find her car missing. Her dad, Gordy, had taken it to the shop to have new tires put on, all fluids changed, and everything prepped for a long trip.

"That was his way of saying it was OK, that I had their blessing."

Her life to that point had been simple. As a girl she spent her time learning about farm life. She helped her dad with every aspect of his tobacco crop, the planting and topping and harvesting, as well as picking stones out of the fields before harvests so that they wouldn't get caught in the machinery. She also knew about hogs and lambs and corn and anything else he needed her to know. Most of her summer days were spent rising by 5:30 a.m. so that she could be in the fields hoeing or picking stones before the heat of the day.

"I learned early on that you had better not ever look bored or you would end up pulling weeds or mowing the yard," Katie laughs.

Gordy fondly remembers those days and what a hard worker Katie was, although he doesn't pretend she enjoyed it. "She used to hate every minute of it, but the madder she got, the harder she worked."

Katie wasn't alone in the fields. She grew up with an older brother, Ryan, and sister, Julie, and a younger brother, Aaron. "In my family you were always talking to someone, whether you wanted to or not."

Not that that was usually the case with Katie as a youngster, at least to anyone outside the family. She was extremely shy, so much so that as a baby the only people who could touch her were her parents. No grandparents, no aunts, no uncles—just mom or dad. At just 17 months old, the family took Katie on a trip to Southern California to visit relatives, and that also meant a trip to Universal Studios. Katie's white-blond hair and fair skin always attracted attention and everyone wanted to touch her or hold her. Katie was OK with the looking, but not the touching.

As one can well imagine, an actor dressed in a Frankenstein costume was no exception to the look-but-don't-touch-rule. "He was huge," Karen says. "He took one look at Katie and was drawn right to her. She never saw him coming."

"He came up from behind her and picked her up," Gordy says. "She took one look at him and just screamed." But the trauma for Katie didn't end there. Gordy took her away from Frankenstein, but decided they needed a photo and returned his screaming child to Frankenstein's arms.

"We knew he wasn't going to hurt her. But Katie didn't know that at the time. I guess we are really bad parents," Karen laughs. She and Gordy share a glance that says it seemed like such an innocent moment at the time, but in retrospect, they realize that it was a significant event for Katie.

Katie has grown more at ease, but she remains far from outgoing. As one of the youngest wives in the garage, she is reluctant to let anyone know her age—she spent her 21st birthday on July 20, 2000, sitting in her and Matt's motor home alone in Long

Pond, Pennsylvania, at Pocono Raceway, while Matt was away at a sponsor appearance.

"I thought, what a loser I am," she laughs. She made the trip home to Wisconsin the following week to celebrate with her friends and family and attempt to buy beer for the first time. "I didn't get carded.

"People do think I am older than I am, and there is rarely a reason to bring it up. It was hard at first trying to fit in, knowing how much younger I was. And I was still trying to get used to the travel and the attention," Katie says.

As Winston Cup racing has grown, so too has the microscope under which the drivers and their families live their lives. In years past, it seemed to take longer for drivers to reach the big time and the limelight. As they were building their careers, these drivers often married high-school sweethearts or friends they had grown up with. Winston Cup had not yet reached the status that it has today, so their courtships remained private.

The next generation of drivers has not been afforded that luxury. Many of these drivers are young and single, so when they bring a friend to the track she is quickly scrutinized.

"I know when we were first dating, I'd walk through the garage and people would point and I'd hear the murmurs, 'Who is that girl?' It's terrible. It is nobody's business, but around here there is a huge wall that you break through [when you transition] from dating to marriage.

"You suddenly become more accepted when you have the ring." Katie and Matt got married the week after the 2000 NASCAR Winston Cup Awards banquet in New York, where Matt accepted his Rookie of the Year honors, and then took a Caribbean cruise before Christmas.

Katie is also adjusting to the fact that the Winston Cup schedule now runs her life, and occasionally her photo is going to show up in racing publications. "I remember the first time I saw my photo in *NASCAR Winston Cup Scene,* I was really uncomfortable. I'm just not comfortable being in the spotlight and I don't want my picture in the paper every week. Now if it means that Matt won every week, that would be OK!"

"I knew he was going to win," Katie says confidently following the first win of Matt's Winston Cup career at Lowe's Motor Speedway in May 2000. "I guess I should say I hoped he would win.

 A 17-month-old Katie being terrified by Frankenstein at Universal Studios in Hollywood, California. Her parents laugh at the incident now, although at the time Katie thought it was quite traumatic. (Katie Kenseth collection)

 Katie at home in Wisconsin at the age of 5. (Katie Kenseth collection)

"You sit there and you say your prayers. More than anything, I didn't want him to make a mistake, like spin out or something crazy that he would never forgive himself for. I was nervous, and when I get nervous I don't watch. I write down the times and I focus on the times so I'm not watching the race or him.

"It was weird, because I don't usually get nervous before a race, but I was talking to Judy Pruett [Scott's wife] at driver intros and I had this stomachache because I was so nervous—it worried me that something bad was going to happen. But then a few hours later we were in victory lane and laughing and smiling and then next thing I know I'm crying because it is just so overwhelming. It sometimes didn't feel real or like it was really us."

Other than the fact that Katie has noticed a few more fans wearing Matt's T-shirts, the win didn't change their life much. Katie didn't take the winnings and go on a shopping spree. They didn't buy a fancy boat or even a Jet Ski. "We got a new refrigerator. That was about it."

Katie has days like the rest of us where "you just want to crawl in a hole and hide from everyone because it never seems like you can say or do the right thing, or you just feel like you are in the way."

But for the most part she greets each day with wide-eyed optimism. She is not only seeing a lot of the racetracks for the first time, but also much of the country. While many of the wives have seen more than enough of places like Talladega, Alabama, and Dover, Delaware, where the sights to see and things to do are limited at best, Katie is still seeing these places with the refreshing perspective that is all too easy to lose in the monotony and rigors of a 36-plus-week race schedule.

"It is still a lot of fun for me," Katie says. "I still laugh at myself not knowing a lot of things about the cars. I remember the first time I went out to driver introductions with Matt and we were talking to someone. I asked Matt afterwards who it was. It was Darrell Waltrip! So when I say I knew nothing about racing when I got here, I mean it. I think that it has really been fun for me to meet the people and have Matt share all of this with me.

"I like to be here, I don't have to be here. I think that is the difference right now. Matt has told me that whenever I decide I don't want to be traveling every week, I don't have to be."

Katie views her role as being Matt's support system. "My job is being here for Matt." That, and handling the books. It didn't take her very long to figure out that racing is more business than sport, and she has taken on all of the bookkeeping for Matt. "Our accountant helps a lot, but Matt doesn't do any of it."

Much to her surprise, she has discovered that she really enjoys doing it. "It's funny because my brother Ryan is an accountant and I told him for years that he was crazy, but now that is what I do nearly every morning. The way I see it now is that meeting Matt showed me something that I would never have picked out for myself."

She has pondered returning to school to get certified as an accountant assistant. Their accountant said she has already learned most of what she would learn in school, so all she would need to do is get that sometimes all-important diploma.

"So I may do that at some point, but I'm happy right now."

She is still most likely to be seen at the track wearing jeans, a white T-shirt, and her favorite hooded sweatshirt. While this shy farm girl continues to avoid the media spotlight, she no longer hides in the motor home. She readily takes on duties to help the Bible Club organize special events. She is one of the many wives who joined Ann Schrader's crusade to obtain a full-time medical liaison to travel the circuit. But above all else, she is an unpretentious girl who loves her husband and their new cat.

"I am just Katie. I don't like to be noticed. The things I enjoy the most are the little things like painting the house, things that we can decide on and do together. That is what is important to me right now."

In the spring of 2001 Katie and Matt welcomed a new member to the family—a yellow kitten named Lars.

Lars?

Katie gestures to the couch where Matt shrugs his shoulders and tosses the question back to her.

"The drummer from Metallica."

So much for the theory that all NASCAR drivers listen to country.

NASCAR BUSCH
DARLINGTON
A NASCAR TRADITION
GTON
TRADITION
Team WINN DIXIE
America's Supermarket
WINN-DIXIE
Valvoline
Superbrand
CRACKIN' GOOD
Chek DRINKS
MAC TOOLS
WINN D
America's S
ROUSH Racing
Superbrand
W D
GAP
GOODYEAR LR-5
AERO
#1
WINN-DIXIE
Chek
MAC TOOLS

ARLENE MARTIN

It was not Arlene's first race, but it was the first time she was going to see Mark compete and it was her first up-close-and-personal view of the pits. She didn't even pretend to take any of it in stride. The first things she noticed were the tires, and in characteristic Arlene fashion, she didn't hesitate to comment.

"The tires were big and fat and they didn't have any tread!

"That to this day has stood out in my mind. I just stood there looking at them and I mean these are big, fat tires, with no tread. I just couldn't get over that and, of course, when I said something they just thought that was the funniest thing, that I didn't know racing tires had no tread."

From that moment on, Arlene began asking questions about racing. She started paying attention to what was going on and why. She was in tune with when Mark was running well and when he wasn't. Then the butterflies began to take control of her stomach whenever she watched him race. There was no way around it, Arlene was falling in love. Maybe even more important than her racing heart was that she had found her best friend.

Only a few months earlier, her other best friend had pronounced that her brother was going to be in town for the holidays.

"My brother's coming home." Glenda Martin had pointed out that fact several times to Arlene. As usual, this time Arlene put her friend off. She felt she had some pretty good reasons for doing so.

Mark Martin was five and a half years her junior.

Arlene had already been married, twice.

"I just hadn't had very good experiences with men and I was about tired of them."

Opposite: The Martins—Mark, Arlene and Matt—celebrate a Busch Series win at Darlington. (Steven Rose/MMP, Inc.)

She was taking a break from the whole dating scene. Her focus was on her four children from her two previous marriages. Glenda had never mentioned Arlene's girls to her brother in her efforts to get him together with Arlene. So Arlene had no idea how Mark might react when he learned about them.

Then there was her attitude about racing.

"I didn't know anything about it, but what little impression I did have, well, it was pretty bad. You have to remember this is Arkansas fifteen years ago. There certainly was no glamour about it. It wasn't popular and I associated it with backward people. Glenda always tried to play it up and point out how great the Daytona 500 was, which was one of the few races on television then. To me it was still racing, you've still got to mess with cars. Who could possibly be interested in watching that? All they do is drive around in a circle."

Another reason not to meet Mark: What would happen if she didn't like him? After all, Glenda was a valued friend in her life.

What's more, Mark no longer lived in Arkansas; his race team was in Wisconsin. Arlene felt certain this just wouldn't work.

Finally at Christmastime in 1983, Arlene relented and agreed to go to Glenda's family's house for dinner.

"He's not going to like me anyway," Arlene thought. "Especially when he finds out I've got kids. Even if he does like me and he thinks he's just going to wine and dine me while he's in town and then leave. Well, that just ain't happening. I was down in the dumps, it was Christmas, I was recently divorced and everything.

"I continued to think the worst before I even got to the house. I really went with the idea that I wasn't going to like him. I was sure he was going to be cocky because he races cars and I wasn't going to put up with that. 'I'll tell him right off that I don't like racing.' That was what I thought."

But nothing went at all as Arlene anticipated.

"He just wasn't even like you would imagine him. He was really quiet, he didn't talk a lot. He didn't really talk about racing at all. He would listen to what we were all talking about. I liked him better than I thought I would. He wasn't cocky; he was real down to earth and friendly. But even when I realized he was real nice, I really had no intention of developing a relationship with him."

Mark had other ideas. He called Arlene almost daily while he

was in town, and while his requests for a date were always denied, the phone conversations grew lengthier. Arlene finally allowed Mark to come over and sit with her at her home for a couple of hours after her daughters had gone to bed.

"He was a gentleman," Arlene says. "He didn't try anything, he never even tried to kiss me."

The relationship continued to develop over the phone after Mark returned to Wisconsin. "We ran my phone bill up and got to know each other that way and became very good friends. I think the reason our relationship ended up working is because he and I became friends before we had a relationship and that just doesn't happen very often."

As their relationship was developing over the phone with them hundreds of miles apart, there were things going on in Mark's life that Arlene didn't fully understand or appreciate until years later. In 1981 Mark owned his team, had won two Winston Cup poles, and had a second- and a seventh-place finish. He was sure he was on his way. He ran for Rookie of the Year in 1982, but got edged out by Geoff Bodine. After experiencing some sponsorship troubles, Mark sold his team and went to drive for J.D. Stacy in 1983.

Unbeknownst to Mark at the time, Stacy, who had fielded two cars and sponsored another five in 1982, was pretty much out of money before Mark even got there. By the end of 1983, just before he met Arlene, Mark's career was in turmoil and he was returning to his ASA roots to regroup. So after spending the holidays in Arkansas, Mark headed back to Wisconsin to prepare for the 1984 season.

Glenda's birthday is at the end of January and Arlene had planned a surprise birthday party. Of course, Mark was invited. The fact that he made the trip didn't surprise Arlene.

"I thought he came to see his sister and family," Arlene says. "At the time I didn't understand that he didn't come home that much. I certainly didn't understand what he was going through at the time with his career. Mark kept things like that to himself. So I didn't at all think he was coming home to see me."

But he was.

Shortly after the party Mark asked Arlene to go to Daytona Speedweeks '84 with him in February. The friendship had developed greatly over the phone and there was no way around the fact that Arlene liked him a lot. She agreed to the trip, still not fully aware of what it meant that Mark was attending this race as a spectator rather than as a competitor.

"I was real oblivious to all of that. I knew he was racing in the Midwest, and this, the Daytona 500, was the first race I had ever gone to in my life and he wasn't in it. But to me he was racing in the Midwest, so that meant he was racing. I could not comprehend the scope of what it meant for us to be in Daytona just walking around among the fans. I didn't know any of the drivers. Cale Yarborough won the Daytona 500 that year and I had never heard of him. The only person whose name I slightly recognized was Richard Petty, but in a trivia game I might have been just as likely to say he was a golfer or a baseball player. I knew Mario Andretti raced cars and I remember wondering why he wasn't racing in that race."

It was April when she would attend an ASA race in Atlanta with Mark and see those treadless tires. That was when she began to understand more not just about racing, but also about the scope of her feelings for Mark.

"I knew I loved him, he was so different than any other man that I had ever been around. Mark and I got to know each other, we were good friends before we got married. I didn't even like the other two [husbands]. I didn't like either one of them as people."

Arlene had married her first husband when she was just 18 years old.

Always fascinated with archeology and history, Arlene imagined that when she went to college she would study history. "I was always intrigued with the way people lived a long time ago. My parents used to make fun of me for that." Arlene also had a fascination with science, so when she enrolled at Arkansas State University she studied biology. Then she met her first husband. He was a senior; she was a freshman. Arlene fell madly in love and the thought of marrying and having a husband and a family and a home became very appealing.

"We were married for four years, I was pregnant with the twins [Heather and Rachel, in 1975], and he comes in and tells me he did not like being married and that one woman was just not enough for him. He couldn't do it anymore.

"I was so heartbroken. I was so in love with him, as much as I could understand love at such a young age. He broke my heart so, I thought I was going to have a nervous breakdown. So stupid me met this other guy, nine years older than I was, and I let him wine and dine me and I married this man on the rebound. He was so opposite from my first husband. I was in love with the idea of being married and having a family. I never let myself get to know him."

Not fully over ending her first marriage, Arlene leaped right into the second one. After all she had children to think about and this man was going to take care of her.

"I was even going back to college. We had moved to Batesville and there was a small college there. I wanted to transfer and go there, finish up my biology degree. I only had one year left. But he talked me out of it. He said I wasn't ever going to have to work. I was so naïve."

Stacy was born two years into that marriage. About the time she turned 2, the flaws in the marriage started to surface. "I got to where I just couldn't stand to see that man pull into the driveway. I started to see a marriage counselor because I was so unhappy. We finally split up, but the actual divorce took so long because of the property disputes. Needless to say, I had had it with men. It wasn't very long after we were finally divorced that I met Mark.

"It had finally clicked in my head that you need to like the person you marry."

• • •

Knowing how much she and Mark loved each other and, and even more than that, that they had a mutual respect for one another as people, didn't keep her knees from buckling as the wedding day approached.

"When we first started talking about marriage in the spring after I started going to races with him, we talked about marrying about a year or even a year and a half ahead. Then it was going to be the following April or May. The next thing I know he is talking about Christmastime. I thought, 'Well, OK,' but then he kept moving it up. When Mark decides he wants to do something, he does it.

"Then he wanted it to be Thanksgiving, but he decided he was probably going to want to race in Jefferson, Georgia, at Thanksgiving, so he said, 'Let's get married at the end of October.'

"I got really nervous then."

Nerves or not, the plans were put in motion. They made reservations to marry at The Peabody Hotel in Memphis. On October 27, 1984, Arlene said, "I do," admittedly somewhat reluctantly.

"I knew I loved Mark and I knew he loved me, but I was so scared of the whole marriage thing. I almost backed out."

Friends had expressed their concerns about how quickly the wedding was happening. They also knew Arlene had never been around racing and had little use for any kind of sport.

As she was stepping into her wedding dress, a friend came in and noticed the difficulty Arlene was having because she was shaking so badly.

"You shouldn't be doing this, you're shaking," she said.

That made Arlene shake even worse, fearing that her friend might be right. Arlene's knees shook all through the reading of the vows. Arlene's history and fear of marriage were only part of her nerves. She had four daughters, ages 8, 11 (the twins), and 13. Mark had never been around kids, and although throughout the courtship he had become a friend to each of them and they all got along from the beginning, there is a difference once the family is truly brought together.

"He probably didn't have a clue what he was getting into with those children. I also knew he wouldn't really understand the scope of what he had gotten into until we got married. Mark never complained. He isn't a very vocal person. Me, I'd have been shouting, 'These kids are driving me crazy.' There is no doubt it was a major adjustment for him, and I will say even to this day I admire him that he handled it like he did. For somebody who was still a kid in a lot of ways and had spent his whole life focused on one thing—racing—that had to be a big thing. What can I say, it worked out!"

As adjusting to parenthood was big for Mark, the realization that racing was now her life was big for Arlene. Not only that, Mark was now trying to rebuild a career that had shown so much promise just a few years before. Drivers don't often experience success in Winston Cup, find themselves without a ride, return to ASA, and then have much of a prayer of making it back to the so-called Big Leagues. But Arlene knew nothing about any of this.

"I went to a few races [while we were dating] and, oh sure, it was fun and you get to go here and you get to go there and I thought, 'Well it's not that bad.' There were only 18 races [in ASA]. I knew Mark was focused on racing, but I don't think I let myself realize how bad he was focused on it, that he wasn't interested in anything else.

"I think it took me well into the third year, and he was Busch racing then, for me to get a full grasp of what was going on and how it was going to be the rest of my life.

"Racing is not normal, you don't have a normal life." Far from it, Arlene says, as she puts on her makeup in the bathroom of their motor home where they sometimes spend more time than they do in their house in Daytona. Arlene laughs at herself putting on her makeup and getting dressed up for the racetrack. "I remember when Kelley Jarrett and I were here in jeans and sweatshirts. It wasn't always the fashion show it is today."

The realization of just how abnormal the racing life can be hit Arlene during the heated 1990 Winston Cup Championship points battle. Mark lost the title to Dale Earnhardt by 26 points. That was the year he had 46 points taken away following his win at Richmond International Raceway in February for having a carburetor spacer that was improperly attached.

"I got so sick of those darn points. Where he finished in the race and the points he got, that affected his personality, that affected the way he was going to act during the week, whether he realized it or not. So in turn it affected me," Arlene says, so exasperated by just the memory of it she has to stop putting on her mascara and take a breath. "I started getting nervous when he raced because I worried about how he was going to finish and how that was going to affect his points. It was [1990], after he lost, I decided I was not going to let those stupid points affect my well-being. It was ridiculous that I spent the whole year on pins and needles and those points would affect how happy or unhappy or how stressed we were. It was then that I realized you had no control over stuff like that, he had no control over why they took those points away from him. You have no control over whether or not the engine breaks or whether or not you hit somebody or they hit you.

"I just decided they were making way too much of a big deal over those fricking points and I was sick of it. I love Mark, of course I want him to do well, but in the grand scheme of things I don't care if he finishes 20th or if he finishes first. I don't care. I'm not going to let any of that bother me because I have too many other things to be appreciative of."

One of those things is their son, Matt. Mark and Arlene were married for seven years before Matt was born in 1991.

Matt has started racing quarter midgets and Arlene never misses a race, but don't mistake that for zealous joy that her son is following in Dad's footsteps.

"I can tell I feel different watching Matt than when I watch Mark. I want to protect Matt more."

No matter how many times he wins, or how much fun he has doing it, Arlene says she hopes that racing is not the path Matt chooses for his life. It's easy for her to be hopeful about that as he sits in the other room watching a John Wayne western, playing with toy soldiers. He is just a kid, and that is the way Arlene likes it.

"Honestly, I don't want him to race, mainly because I know how hard it is and what it takes away from your life. It is so easy to get wrapped up in something like racing that you forget the things that are really important in life, and I don't want him to be like that.

"He is at the point where he could like it and he could not. He races his quarter midgets, but he talks about how he is going to be a marine. He's into his soldiers and he's real into the Civil War and World War II right now. So racing is just fun. I want it to stay that way for him. Of course, I'll be fine with whatever he decides. Besides, he may not be any good at it."

But less than a year after Arlene made those comments at Bristol in 2000, Matt's casual quarter-midget racing took a decidedly more serious turn. The Quaker Oats Company provided sponsorship from its Cap'n Crunch and Life Cereal brands. Matt was even featured on cereal boxes. Citgo and Gatorade also signed on as associate sponsors for the 2001 season, during which Matt raced twice a week at New Smyrna Speedway Quarter Midget Raceway and at Mid Florida in Apopka, both tracks in Florida.

Matt continues to learn and improve and Arlene says he holds his own, but quickly points out that Matt began racing at age 7. A lot of his competitors began at 5. "Those two years make a big difference at that age."

"I really didn't like the idea much," Arlene says. "I guess I've gotten used to it and he's gotten better. Mark helped build that track at New Smyrna and he has been with him at his races on Wednesday nights. That's been a lot of fun."

Arlene may be attending more midget races than Winston Cup races these days, but she is still by Mark's side as often as she can be. However, you won't find her on top of the truck watching practice or out on pit road for qualifying. Arlene spends most of her time in the motor home relaxing and steering clear of the hubbub.

"I just keep to myself and a lot of times I don't get to the track until Saturday," she adds. "I don't know. I think I have spent enough years in the garage that it is fine for me now to show my support from behind the scenes."

Touchstone Energy
300
CELLULARONE racing
NASCAR BUSCH GRAND NATIONAL DIVISION
CELLULARONE
Touchstone Energy® 300
WINNER
April 15, 2000
NASCAR BUSCH GRAND NATIONAL DIVISION
CELLULARONE racing

Andrea Nemechek

John Nemechek was smiling as he headed out the door en route to Homestead, Florida, for the NASCAR Craftsman Truck Series race in March 1997.

He continued to smile as he rubbed a hand across his sister-in-law's tummy. "Oh my God, your belly is getting so big." Andrea and Joe Nemechek were expecting their first child in three months.

Andrea brushed John's hand away with a laugh and wished him well as she and Joe prepared to leave for the Busch Series race in Las Vegas. That would be the final exchange between Andrea and her brother-in-law, who was also one of her closest friends.

She was sitting outside at the back of the team hauler when Joe's crew chief came out and told Andrea that John had been in a terrible accident in the truck race. "Andrea, it's bad, you'd better come into the lounge." Stunned, she followed him to the lounge at the front of the hauler to see the television coverage. She watched in silence as it showed a replay of the wreck, which at first didn't appear to be too bad. From the angle they showed, it wasn't clear to Andrea whether he had hit the wall on the driver's side of the truck. The helicopter arrived quickly to take John to the hospital. At that point, the information being relayed through the television broadcast was minimal.

"I had to go find Joe before people started asking him about it. He didn't know anything yet, of course, I didn't know much, but I still knew it wasn't good. I felt it," Andrea says. "I kept telling myself, 'They've airlifted people out before and they were OK. Maybe he's just knocked out.'"

Andrea told Joe what little she knew and tried to act hopeful.

"I think he's OK though," she said to her husband before he got into his race car.

NASCAR tried to reassure the Nemecheks, and the couple said a prayer for John before Joe got into the car. But during the race NASCAR officials let Andrea know the situation was grim. After the race, Andrea and Joe headed to the NASCAR trailer where officials gave the Nemecheks use of the private office so they could use the phone.

They tried to prepare themselves, but there was no way to brace for this kind of news.

"They said he might not make it through the night," Andrea says. "We were devastated. The first person I remember seeing as we left the trailer was Kelley Jarrett. She lost her brother the year before. She was just right there and said, 'Andrea, are you all OK? I'm here if you need me.'

"NASCAR flew us [to Miami] on their jet. It was such a long flight and we were sure he was going to be gone when we got there.

"He was unconscious when we got to the hospital. They had him on machines and he was still breathing, so we thought he was going to be all right. He may not be back to the old John, but he's going to be OK."

John had every imaginable tube in his body. Incapable of moving himself, he was strapped to a bed that moved his arms and legs to keep a flow of circulation. His brain stem had been severed, and at first they were uncertain if it was reparable or not.

"Martha (Joe and John's mother) is Catholic. I learned all of those prayers and we'd sit around and we'd hold hands and we'd pray," Andrea says.

After five days, the doctors' tests showed a complete loss of brain activity.

"You could see the tears in [the doctor's] eyes. We knew John was gone. 'He's brain dead,' he told us. 'There's nothing we can do.' It was awful. It was awful. Terrible." Andrea's thoughts drifted off at the memory as the tears began to surface.

John remained on life support until they could remove and donate his organs.

"The hardest part for me was watching John's girlfriend, Harriett. I kept thinking what if this was Joe, what would I do? It was devastating to all of us. She wanted to marry him. This had become her life, like it had become mine.

"She didn't get to see him before the race. That is the thing she regrets the most. She was scoring for the team so she was up in the scoring stand. He waved at her. 'I'd give anything to have that moment back,' she told me."

Joe's parents weren't sure if they could ever go racing again. Martha even asked Joe if he would give up racing.

"Mom, that's something I love. John wouldn't want me to give it up," Joe said.

• • •

Andrea's comfort level with the sport was severely shaken as well.

"Every time a wreck happened, it scared me half to death. I told Joe, 'Anytime you are in a wreck, you have got to come on the radio and tell me that you are OK.' I can't handle not knowing. I couldn't go through that every race or I wouldn't be able to go racing anymore. It was very hard. It still is hard." Andrea stops and looks out the window at the sun glistening on Lake Norman.

When Andrea got pregnant she wanted to know if she and Joe were having a boy or a girl. "When I had my first sonogram they kept telling me they weren't sure, but they thought I was having a girl. I wanted to know so bad, there was no way I could wait until the end. Then just before John's accident we found out it was a boy. I think that was meant to be. The Lord had a part in that. He needed John, so I guess he gave us a gift [in baby John Hunter] and it has been the most wonderful thing in the world.

"It has helped the whole family get through the tragedy. You never get over it. The pain lessens, but you still miss him every single day. The saddest part is that John never got to see John Hunter. John and Joe had totally different personalities and the funny thing is that John Hunter is just like John, always laughing, smiling, full of life. He has John in him somewhere and he has filled that void so much, especially with Joe's mom and dad.

"You realize that life is so short. I could die tomorrow. I try, when I get angry about something, like with racing and your engine blowing up or something, [to remember that] it's not a big deal. Yes, you want to do well and you want to win, but there are worse things."

Potentially much worse.

In November 1999, Andrea was eight months pregnant with their second child. The Nemechek clan had just flown home from Homestead, the track at which John had lost his life. Joe had conquered it with a win in the Busch race. The Nemechek family would now have a positive memory of Homestead. Everyone—Joe and his father in the front, Martha, Andrea, and John Hunter in the back—piled into the car to go home. In less than five minutes, everything changed.

"The road that used to go straight now went into a 90-degree turn," Andrea recalls.

Joe was driving. He had two choices—hit heavy construction equipment head on or take his chances with a swerve into the ditch. Joe opted for the ditch. The car flipped twice. Andrea was in the back in between Martha and John Hunter in his car seat. She was the only one without a seatbelt and the only one injured. She suffered a couple of broken ribs, a collapsed lung, a cut on her head, a broken shoulder blade, and a sprained knee. More than anything else, Andrea was concerned about her unborn baby. She was fine.

"I was lucky, with her being so well developed. They are pretty well packed in there by then. Had I not been that far along, I probably would have lost her." Blair was born the next month, the day after Christmas. Andrea smiles as she glances over at the ottoman in the Nemechek's expansive living room where Blair is playing and cooing joyfully.

Blair is just one reason Andrea finds to still smile. Despite John's death and her own accident, that smile is ever-present; it was one of the reasons *Winston Cup Illustrated* selected her as one of NASCAR's most beautiful people.

"I didn't know until a friend of Joe's mom called and said, 'Hey, tell Andrea she's one of the hot women of NASCAR.' I thought, 'Oh come on, you're full of it.'"

When some of the women from the race shop called and confirmed it, "I was

very honored. I don't know why they picked me, but it is nice to know that people think of you."

Born in Lexington, Kentucky, in March 1966, Andrea considers herself more a native of Myrtle Beach, South Carolina. Her parents divorced when she was a baby. She and her mother lived in Nashville for a little while before she moved to Myrtle Beach, but she doesn't recall any of it.

Andrea always had a special bond with her father, and even though she had fairly frequent visits with him, she says, "I missed him whenever we weren't together. It was hard, but now we are as close as you can possibly be."

After graduating from the University of South Carolina–Columbia with a degree in retail management, her need to be near her father drew her to Orlando. And it was her dad, Frank, who decided she needed to meet the son of some friends of his whom he had known ever since he moved to Lakeland, Florida, when Joe was just a boy.

"My dad and a bunch of other businessmen put together this Margarita Ball every year, usually in November or December. You get all dressed up and bring toys for needy children to get in. He was really good friends with Joe's parents and he told them that they needed to come to this event. He was setting Joe and me up, of course."

Andrea fortunately didn't take a date to the ball that year (1988), but she had a girlfriend there with her. She was introduced to Joe, who is shy in such situations. He's not the kind of person who goes out of his way to create something to say if he doesn't have anything on his mind. "We made some small talk, but Joe didn't seem to have much to say, so after a little while I went off with my friend.

"The next thing I know, he's kind of hanging out behind me. We start talking a little bit. He asked me if his tie matched his suit. Soon we were laughing and having a really good time and we ended up dancing almost all night.

"The next night he called and he brought me roses."

Joe was racing Late Model stocks at the time, but Andrea couldn't even have begun to tell you what that meant.

"I had never seen a race in my life. Even though Myrtle Beach had a speedway, it was not what we did. The beach is what we did."

But the races were short in that series and held at night, "and it was fun. We had a great time." Soon Joe moved up to the All-

Pro series and Andrea still tagged along sometimes, but she had a job. Andrea was working for a chain of sporting goods stores, helping to set up new stores and training the employees all over the region. It was a good job and she enjoyed it. So in 1990 when Joe moved to North Carolina to race in the Busch series, she didn't immediately follow.

"That was really hard. I tried to get up there as much as I could, but it was really hard."

When Joe raced at Volusia County in South Carolina later that year, there was no question, at least on the part of Andrea's father, Frank, that Joe would stay with him while in town.

"The morning after he arrived he asked me to marry him! It was that simple," Andrea says.

"I never saw it coming. I mean we were living so far apart and I just thought that was the furthest thing from his mind. I don't think he had planned it out because he didn't have a ring or anything. It was pretty far from my mind too, quite honestly, but I'm really glad he did it."

Andrea made the move north and lived with Joe and his brother John before she and Joe got married. After the wedding they all shared an apartment for a couple of years until she and Joe could build a house. "Of course, I complained, 'Gosh, I have to take care of two men.' John loved to cook. He loved to grill out and make stuff. We'd always be the ones in the kitchen getting dinner ready and Joe would be on the couch watching TV or reading or something. He doesn't want to have anything to do with the kitchen. We were a family and I am so grateful for that time we had together."

During all this time, like it or not, Andrea was learning about racing. She took a job with a Barrett Shoes Store in Burlington when she first moved to Salisbury, North Carolina, and made the commute—more than an hour each way—every day. In 1992 Joe bought a Busch shop in Mooresville, North Carolina, and needed somebody to run the office. Andrea was glad to take the job.

"At that time it really didn't faze me at all to give up my retail career. I wanted to be with Joe and I was so grateful for the chance to travel with him and help him in any way that I could."

Since then she admits there are times when she thinks about the amount of time she spent in college studying and the work she put in to further her position in retail, and wishes she had a career of her own. "Our life is his life. Everything we do revolves around Joe. Sometimes I think, what would we do if something happened to him? I mean, we have tried to be smart with our investments and stuff, and you don't want to think like that, but I do wonder sometimes if I would be able to find a job after this long out of the workforce. You really give up your life to be married to somebody in racing at this level. But you make the choice to keep your marriage and family together."

While racing has brought her many joys and has afforded her and her family a nice home on Lake Norman in North Carolina, it is hardly a dream life around which to raise a family.

Joe was injured early in the summer of 2001, which meant several weeks at home while he recovered. Andrea admits she may have enjoyed it a little too much, and she has thoughts of a future that does not have her traveling every weekend.

"It was so nice. Joe wasn't stressed and we got to do weekend stuff like go outside and play and have a normal weekend. If Joe had the chance to be a team owner and not a driver and we could spend more time at home, I would really like that. The traveling is so hard and draining when you have kids."

But John Hunter already has visions of changing that stay-at-home plan. "He already wants to race so bad. It scares me. I admit I don't like the idea of him racing at all. The life is so hard. If he is involved I'm going to want to be there, but I don't want to travel for the rest of my life. Besides, there are already enough other ways for him to get hurt, why does he have to add to it?"

With the nature of the Winston Cup schedule, there is no way to avoid returning to the site of John's accident each year, and it has yet to get easier.

"Joe's parents didn't go with us [the first race after the accident]. It was so hard. The press was all over Joe and wanted to know what he felt. We had gone to the track right after John's death to see what had happened and where it happened. We tried to take some time with it then, when we were alone, and tried to find some peace with it.

"When we went down for the Homestead race, we just kept telling ourselves that we could do it. Joe didn't really show a lot of emotion about it. He did win and that meant so much to everyone. But while we were there, we were just in a daze the whole weekend. We were there to race, get it over with, and go home."

Andrea continues to get nervous before every race, right when Joe climbs into the car. There has been only one race where she didn't have the opportunity to see Joe before he got in the car—Indianapolis in 2000—but she doesn't intend to let that happen ever again.

"I always try to see Joe before he gets in the car. I just want to make sure I'm there. Once the race starts and they get spread out I'm not so nervous, unless he's leading and doing really good, then I get really nervous.

"When we won the race at New Hampshire, I didn't know if we would win or not, but we were a ways from the end and the tears just started flowing. I kept saying, 'I can't get like this. I can't get so emotional. What if he doesn't win and I'm sitting here crying and people will think I'm crying because of that.' So I tried to stay as calm as I could, but I don't know how calm a person can stay in that situation. So I told myself that the Lord was watching over everything and it was all going to be OK: 'So Andrea, get the butterflies out and let him enjoy his day.'"

Joe did win and they all enjoyed their day more than Andrea can even begin to describe.

"I think my one wish for everyone in that garage would be for them all to get to experience that once in their careers. It is unbelievable."

Left: Andrea and Joe share a wedding-day kiss. (Andrea Nemechek collection)

CREW CARE
CENTER
Coca-Cola
Goody's
ESPN

JACKIE PEGRAM

She climbs out of bed every day with more energy than most of us could hope to muster even several cups of coffee into our best day. It is impossible for anyone, especially a child, to meet her and leave untouched. Her energy and smiles are infectious and seemingly constant.

Jackie Pegram, 57, is on this earth to teach children the Bible. She will tell you that, and anyone who knows her will agree. Known to all in racing as Miss Jackie, it has been less than ten years since she began the Bible study program for children with Motor Racing Outreach. But she and the program have become an essential part of life on the road for the drivers and their families.

Once you're infected with her smile and breathless energy, it is hard to imagine her being anything but a ray of sunshine and happiness. However, for much of her life, her energy went into simply surviving.

Jackie Willis grew up in Newport News, Virginia, the daughter of a Navy docking pilot. Her mother was a doll artist and "she played a lot of bingo," Jackie says. Her father, Adrian, was an alcoholic and was abusive to her mother and her older brother, but never to her.

"He drank on the weekends. It never affected his profession and my mother consistently said, 'You know he doesn't mean it.' That's what people do in that setting, and certainly in those days you didn't talk about it and you didn't leave.

"My daddy was a sweet man, but alcohol made him mean and he would go into these rages on the weekends. Every Monday or Tuesday morning he got us together and he promised, 'I won't do it again.'

"I was so sad and so scared that my daddy would hurt my mother."

Jackie also carried a tremendous amount of guilt because Adrian would openly hurt and be mean to her mother and brother and then talk about how wonderful she was. "That was the worst. So I lived this kind of weird secretive life. I had a real need as a child for somebody to help me in my sadness."

Jackie filled that need in church with a Sunday-school teacher named Esther. Surprisingly, Jackie did not come from a strong Christian family. Her mother took her to Sunday school occasionally, but Jackie became a Christian at the age of 12 on her own.

"There was a lady in Sunday school and she taught me a lot about Christ and how much he loved me. Esther was her name and I think that is why Esther is my favorite book in the Bible. She told me that God never left me. The Bible says so and that was very important to me.

"My daddy would be pitching fits and throwing stuff and threatening to kill my mother. Me and the Lord would be in my bedroom. He was with me. I didn't understand all of the faith thing then, I just knew that I could talk to Him and He never left me."

During her teens she began attending a Baptist church with all of her friends, and that is where her love of the scripture was born. It was also during her teen years at

Princess Ann High School that she met the man who would be her first love and first husband.

She was pretty, she was popular, and she had a lot of friends. "Of course with my energy level, you know I was president of stuff and I sold lots of doughnuts and raised money for all kinds of things for school and church. I partied with everyone, but I was always the one who drove home … the one that counseled everybody."

When she met Bubba he was dating her best friend, Molly. "I dated lots of people, but I never liked any of them. I was just everybody's friend. I guess I just wasn't really romantically inclined then." But when Molly went out of town one weekend, Bubba called Jackie and invited her to go to the movies with him. She saw no real reason why she shouldn't go.

"Well, I fell in love, I mean slam, in love! It was amazing!"

Molly didn't stay mad very long and Jackie continued to see Bubba. "He had this great personality and I just loved him, I still love him to this day. He was also very needy and I thought I could fix him."

She graduated from high school a year early and enrolled at Meredith College in 1964 with the intention of becoming a

They began teaching Bible study to crew members and their families at several of the race shops in Mooresville, North Carolina. That was great, but Jackie's first race-track experiences at Busch Series races were not. "The first couple of races, I had no idea what I was going to do all day. I had no place to be, no one to talk to and just nothing at all to do."

This was in the early '90s. Only a very small handful of drivers had motor homes and the tracks didn't have a specific spot to put them. Jackie tried to get to know people, but there weren't very many women around. She noticed that the few that were there had children with them.

"I told Ron I saw children there. And I knew that if they were at the track they weren't going to Sunday school, because even with the Busch race on Saturday, they were driving home late that night or early the next morning and they were not getting up to go to Sunday school."

She hadn't taught kids in about seven years, and then the environment had been much more conducive to study than was the back of a car or trailer. But Jackie planted herself in the back of Phil Parsons' trailer and attempted to teach Sunday school to Phil Parsons', Robert Pressley's, and Hut Stricklin's children.

"This was the back of a trailer, not a big hauler like they have now. It was so loud you couldn't hear, but we did it."

Jackie began lobbying for a motor home and hit a wall at every turn. She was able to talk one company into loaning her one for a race; it was so ideal that Ron broke down and bought one for them to use. They scrimped and saved, and for the first couple of years they bought everything for the children's program themselves. After two and half years they couldn't afford it anymore, and had to go back to borrowing whenever they could.

"I wasn't sure we were going to be able to keep going, but we had a couple dozen kids coming every weekend by then and it was great for them." Not one to keep quiet about the needs of MRO and the children, Jackie voiced her concerns in front of the right people at the Atlanta race in 1996.

"This woman came up to me and was so excited about what I was doing with the children, she asked where I did it. Well, you know me. I told her and I told her I didn't know what we were going to do. She grabbed her husband by the arm and told him to get us a motor home."

Her husband was a vice president with Fleetwood, the motor home manufacturer.

The program has since exploded. The tracks have stepped up and provided areas for MRO and the drivers to be separated from the infield. And the kids have a regular neighborhood with their friends and church—it just happens to change locations every weekend.

Jackie averages twenty-four students per day throughout the weekend, but can have as many as forty at some races. Her focus is on the young children, but they are not forgotten as they grow. With the growth of the sport and the support of the program, MRO now has a staff that affords them the ability to have ministers for a youth group, as well. They take camping trips in Pennsylvania and do other things teens enjoy.

It is highly unlikely that, anywhere else, you could throw together thirty to fifty-plus people of different religious backgrounds and teach their children about Jesus without repercussions.

"Never has a person said to me, 'I do not like what you taught.' Never has anyone questioned it. It is amazing. Churches and people that I talk to cannot believe it, especially from such a wide variety of people. We have had favor in this community unlike anything I have ever seen.

"I think part of it is they see how hard I work and how much I truly love the children. When their kids leave MRO for the day they leave laughing and singing. How can you argue with that? I am so careful with what I teach the children because their parents have put so much trust in me, also because children will take what you say as the 100 percent truth. My passion is the Bible and that is what I teach, the scripture."

Even now, as the demands of the schedule grow for everyone involved, Jackie still takes the time on Monday to write to every child that was in Bible Club the weekend before.

Jessica Waltrip, Darrell and Stevie's daughter, is now a teenager, and she told Jackie that she still has every one of those letters. Jackie says, "That is one of those things that makes all the late nights and the struggles to get here worthwhile.

"I don't get a lot of letters, or a lot of hoopla, but Mark Martin said to me once that he could never pay me back for what I have done for his little boy. As a teacher, those are the things that keep you going."

PATTIE PETTY

Pattie Petty stands in the pits awaiting the start of the Winston Cup race at Dover Downs in June 2000. Her yellow-blond bob is set off strikingly by her black mock turtle-neck. The midday June sun forces a squinted smile onto her face that, from a distance, looks like typical Pattie. But up close, the eyes are weary, the smile not so quick to come, the tears much quicker.

"I'm just taking it one day at a time," she chokes. "It is all I can do."

It has been just less than a month since Pattie and Kyle buried their oldest son, Adam, at the age of 19. Adam Petty was killed in May as a result of injuries suffered in a crash during Busch Series practice at New Hampshire International Speedway.

Prior to Adam's accident, Pattie was splitting her time between horseback riding with daughter Montgomery Lee, nicknamed Gummy, and overseeing the construction of Adam's house on the family farm. She also was spearheading the efforts to bring a Paul Newman Hole in the Wall Gang camp for critically ill children, to be called Victory Junction, to North Carolina. That left little time to spend entire weekends at the race-track.

The weekend of May 12, 2000, there was no Winston Cup Series race. Kyle was in England with Montgomery Lee, 14, sharing in the equestrian activities usually reserved for Mom. Adam's house was nearly complete, requiring only a few personal touches. Just before leaving for Loudon, Adam had moved his clothes from his parents' house to his new house. Pattie could think of no better way to spend the weekend than shopping for furniture for her son's new home.

She had scoured antique shops and made her way to Rose Furniture in High Point, North Carolina, when her cell phone rang. It was certainly not the call she could have

Opposite: Pattie joins Kyle for pre-race ceremonies. (Steven Rose, MMP, Inc.)

ever imagined getting when she cheerfully answered her phone.

"It was a NASCAR official," Pattie says. "Adam had crashed during practice and hit the wall really hard."

He was gone.

"I needed to get Kyle back home as quickly as possible and he had to tell Gummy. We didn't know how to do that. Those moments, that whole time is such a blur and was so unbelievable. There was pain, there was anger, there was disbelief." Seeing a great need for his help, Pattie and Kyle's other son, Austin, then 18, took charge, assuming the arduous task of the details, funeral arrangements, phone calls, and the like.

The racing community was stunned, and as always in times of tragedy, it pulled together. Gummy spoke emotionally about her brother at the funeral, and in the days that followed, Kyle and Pattie thanked everyone for their support and for respecting their privacy during this unimaginably difficult time. The daily outpouring of love and sympathy through cards, letters, and flowers from the fans and racing community were a comfort.

But eventually things began to change. Time passed and cards stopped coming. Pattie wasn't really surprised by that, after all people move on with their lives and that's OK. Worse was that people started looking the other way as they walked past the Pettys in the garage.

"I am ashamed to admit I have been one of those people," former champion turned television commentator Benny Parsons said as he and Pattie chatted in Bristol in August 2000. "Because I don't know what to say. I can't say I know what you are going through because I don't, and I don't know what to say so I say nothing, and I hate that I have become one of those people."

"Say that," Pattie says. "That has been so hard because I know people don't know what to say to us, but telling us that is better than looking the other way."

Adam's death has also made it much more difficult for Pattie and Kyle to be apart. Pattie no longer fits the race weekend into the rest of her schedule, now she structures her routine around it to avoid time apart from Kyle.

"Kyle and I are more uncomfortable away from each other. It seems that when we are with other people or without each other, everyone is so uncomfortable, they don't know what to say or whether or not to bring it up or say anything at all. Kyle and I find ourselves trying to make everyone else comfortable. So we are better when we are together, we can talk about it or not talk about it. We can just be.

"I've become very much a follower. That has never been who I was before, but I am just not in the state of mind to make any decisions anymore." The reality of those words seems to baffle Pattie even as she speaks them. To outsiders, she still carries herself with dignity and grace and a strength that is to be admired. It helps her to continue to focus on Kyle and on helping their kids fulfill their dreams.

Austin and Gummy made the decision to have Kyle take over Adam's seat in the No. 45 car and drive it for the rest of the season.

"For them there was no one else," Pattie says. "The team rallied around Kyle and supported that decision. It's been nice to feel such a part of that team. I feel Adam is still there in a lot of ways. Believe it or not, probably the most peace that Kyle and I have is when we are with that team."

Gummy continues to focus her energies on her horses. "She is as focused with her horses as Adam was with his race car. She wants to be a champion and there is no doubt that she will be." Indeed, Gummy went on to win the World Championship in Western Pleasure at the American Quarter Horse Youth Association World Championships in August 2001.

After Adam's death, Austin went to Florida to spend the summer working at one of Paul Newman's Hole in the Wall Gang camps. He was seeking a direction in his life. Bringing one of these camps to North Carolina has been very impor-

tant to his family, so he wanted to learn more.

"He spent all summer learning how to work with these kids," Pattie says. "He turned his hair yellow early in the summer because at that time his group was the yellow group, and then [in August] he was with the terminally ill children, so he shaved his head to look like them. I think this camp is going to happen quicker because Austin is so involved with the project. He is so focused on getting it here." Victory Junction is scheduled to open in 2004.

"My kids are incredible."

All of it is a credit to Kyle, if you ask Pattie. "Kyle has such a big heart and he values people so much, he has passed that along to our kids. They are him."

Gummy's eyes light up at the sound of her mom's raspy Southern drawl sweeping through the barn. "We are so close," Gummy beams. "I've gotten to where I tell her everything."

Pattie locates the stall Gummy is using as a tack room at the East Coast National Horse Show in Lexington, Virginia. She nearly topples over as her teenage daughter leaps into her mom's arms.

"So tell me about how the show is going," Pattie inquires, still holding her daughter tightly.

Gummy erupts with a list of who has done what where and why her pattern got messed up there, "But, oh, I got a trophy for this, come see …." The pair look like sisters as they trot through the barn, arms wrapped around each other's waists, heads touching, laughter reverberating down the row of stalls.

Although Pattie sat Gummy up on a horse before she turned 5 years old, Gummy didn't begin her showing career until she was 13. The somewhat delayed start didn't seem to have an adverse affect on her. "She won everything there was to win," Pattie says. "We were at the Quarter Horse awards banquet [in 1999]. It was almost embarrassing. She was high points youth, amateur … everything in the state of North Carolina, she won rookie titles and won every all-around title there was to win and then she was still voted Sportsman of the Year by her peers."

Pattie beams with pride as she relays the story and watches Gummy prepare for the day's events, trying to select the appropriate colored jacket.

"I think that is pretty incredible. When Jeff Gordon came in here and was beating everyone here at the age of 22, do you think they would have voted him Sportsman of the Year?"

Even more remarkable than the actual titles is what Gummy, completely of her own volition, did with some of the money she won.

A young boy named Jason was the rider to beat on any given day, until Gummy came along. They were acquaintances, but the keenness of the competition meant they were not really buddies. Jason's family farm was in eastern North Carolina, a part of the state that was ravaged by Hurricane Floyd in the fall of 1999. They lost everything.

Montgomery Lee stared with big round eyes at her two checks for $500 apiece. Her parents figured she was thinking about the new show saddle that she had been saving for. Instead Gummy quietly asked if it was OK if she gave her money to Jason and his family.

"They don't have anything, they lost everything, and $1,000 could help them," she said to her mom and dad as their eyes filled with tears.

"She said it without a lot of thought … and she did it quietly. "She didn't stand up and say, 'Let me present you with this check.' She didn't go around telling all her friends, 'Hey, guess what I did.' She wasn't thinking even one bit of Gummy," Pattie recalls. "I don't know that that was a lesson I've ever taught her. That was just pure heart of Kyle. It was the most incredible night, because I realized that everything Kyle stands for and everything he has taught them is there."

That, maybe more than anything else, is what Pattie wants most for her kids and her-self, to be like Kyle.

She's hardly considered quiet or shy, but you are hard pressed to get Pattie to say much about herself. Kyle, the kids, horses, Kyle's Charity Ride, the Victory Junction camp, she gladly prattles on for hours about such topics. But when it comes time to talk about Pattie Petty, it isn't so much that she has things she'd rather not reveal, so much as she would just rather you hear about the impact Kyle has had on her life.

"I have learned more from Kyle Petty than I have ever learned from my parents, from any book, or any life experience."

Patty Huffman had been happily working her way through graduate school as a Winston girl on the weekends at Camel GT races. It was fun and entertaining, and she got to travel and earned decent money to boot.

"They paid me $100 a day," she recalls. "I could leave on Thursday, get all my school work done and go to the races on Friday, Saturday, and Sunday. I was able to do my job at the track during the day and then go back to the motels at night and do my studies. It worked out really well and I was making $300 a weekend. That was, and still is, good money."

After about a year and a half of this nice routine, working about eighteen to twenty weekends per year while studying for a doctorate in child psychology and teaching school in Randolph County, the folks at RJ Reynolds asked Patty to move to Winston Cup. Patty was hesitant even before she knew that it would require an additional day per week and a lot more weekends per year. She was comfortable where she was. "I told them I couldn't do four days because of school, but they weren't really listening and I tried it anyway."

• • •

Her first event was at Nashville, and after working at road-racing venues like Laguna Seca in California and Sebring in Florida, Nashville came as a bit of a shock. "There were no toilets!" She was planning to call the friend who had gotten her into this whole mess. "I was going to kill her."

There, as she got out of the car, was a teenager on crutches. Kyle Petty, 16, had broken his leg playing high school football.

"I think you live near us. Don't you have horses?" Kyle asked. "My mom and dad are looking for some horses for my little sister."

"Well, tell them to come see me. I've got some really nice horses," Patty responded.

Kyle ended up visiting Patty while his parents were off buying horses from someone else. A friendship was in bloom. Kyle would visit, sometimes with his sisters, and they would all go horseback riding. He would go to horse shows with her. There was nothing more to it. She continued her work as a Winston girl. "At the time there was such a stigma about dating the competitors. You didn't stop and talk to people for any length of time; you're a friend to everybody, but a close buddy to nobody."

About a year later, Kyle began calling Patty. Patty found that a series of thoughts would pass through her mind: "I think he likes me. This is not good. His mother—what is she going to think? I'm so much older than he is. This is not a neat little package." She is eight years older than Kyle. "Can't I just lie and say we went to high school together and that we are the same age! That would be easier.

"I told him not to call me anymore. And he quit calling me. I guess it was about a month and I hadn't seen or talked to him and I realized how much I missed him. I really missed his company."

They ran into each other again at the track and the attraction was undeniable. "I started to worry about my job, and at the time I was really enjoying the money. I was just about to finish school, but he started coming to visit again and we realized we were more than just friends.

"I taught school in a county nearby and here I am going to high school football games with Kyle. It was a very ugly picture at the time.

"Going to the prom was really weird. It was odd, but it was very nice weird. I can remember thinking, 'How do I dress?' They dressed one way and I dressed another, so it was strange. When I look back, I wonder what I would do if one of my sons brought home an older woman. I would question it. Kyle wouldn't."

Kyle's family never questioned the relationship, or if they did, they never let Patty know it. It certainly never fazed Kyle. "Kyle was very mature. He was raised with grown men at the racetrack, he was never raised with kids, so he never acted his age. So it never affected me. It affected everybody looking at us. The remarks did occasionally bother me a little bit, but they never seemed to bother him and I really began to love him to the point that I didn't care. I stopped concerning myself with what other people thought. I knew what we had. We became such good friends and the rest came later and that's a good thing, I think. You can really love somebody and not like them, and I think you had better like them if you are going to marry them. I feel so blessed

that I got to marry my best friend."

Kyle was 18 when he proposed to Patty. "We went out to the barn at his parents' to feed the horses and I was pouring the feed, and I looked down and there was a diamond in the feed. The mare was fixing to eat it! I grabbed it. We laughed. It was just really cute and really fun."

They married on February 4, 1979. That is when Patty became Pattie. "Honestly, I don't mind how anybody spells it. When we got married, my name seemed kind of funny the way it was spelled with the two Ys, so I changed it to P-A-T-T-I-E."

Marrying into stock car racing's first family didn't carry the perks then that it does now. "There wasn't a whole lot to be in awe of back then, as far as racing and being a family went. Somebody new coming in now can see the jets, the buses, the big houses, the stuff, the material things. That stuff wasn't there.

"Kyle's mother loaded up gobs of food—cooked all night Saturday night—threw ten or twelve people into a van, because you only had one car to travel in and you could only get one car pass if you were lucky. And you loaded everybody in a van and all this food and this is what she did every week and this is what the other wives did every week. You lived in the car for a day and you fed your children in the dirt. So this wasn't really something that you wanted to do."

That was also a time when women were being told they had better have children before they turned 30, that it wasn't safe beyond then. Pattie got pregnant with Adam 9 months after she and Kyle were married, and had Austin 16 months after Adam. It was not an easy time.

"The money wasn't there. We lost our home in Randleman. We just couldn't afford it. We lost everything we had. We moved to my father's house at Badin Lake and lived there for several years until we could get back on our feet."

Money was very tight and Kyle's time was being pulled away from his family. Sponsorship dollars were just beginning to grow, as was sponsors' and owners' impatience as they demanded performance immediately. Kyle struggled through lost rides and lost sponsorships, all of which took a tremendous toll on his family life.

"It was a big strain on our marriage. It was a good thing that I liked and loved my husband. But I didn't like everything he did through those times. I didn't like everything he did in response to the pressure, the stress. He didn't include me. He isolated me."

Adam and Austin were entering their pre-teen years and Montgomery Lee was just starting school. "That is not an easy time with children."

It is important to keep in mind that although the money had improved by the early '90s, Kyle and Pattie were not wealthy. It was still very uncommon to have motor homes and jets and travel every week together. The Motor Racing Outreach community center, which provides a haven for the children and encourages families to be together, wasn't on the scene yet. It is probably safe to say that bringing the family along was not only not encouraged, but outright discouraged.

"You were left alone a lot. Your husband couldn't take you with him and then it almost became easier for him not to even try to take you along. We barely got passes for ourselves, much less the children. It was awful. [NASCAR] did not want us here, so they didn't make any effort for us to be here. Our husbands were caught in a catch-22, because if they helped us get in here, they were going against NASCAR. Darrell Waltrip was one of the few that fought for [his wife] Stevie to get in.

"There were many, many demands with three little children…[Kyle] was gone all the time.

"If a wife ever tells you that she doesn't feel second [to racing] at times, she is lying. I felt I had no self worth. It was a huge struggle for me to keep my perspective. I became very negative, and that was probably very difficult for Kyle to deal with because I had always been very optimistic. Basically, human beings want to feel secure. At that time I felt very insecure. I felt very vulnerable. I felt very left out. From the time Adam was 10 until he was 15, years just went by. I was just biding time."

Pattie felt so left out that she even considered leaving Kyle.

"Yeah, I thought about it. I knew I had a career. My children were at that age where I could have gone to work during the day and had some self satisfaction that I was a valuable individual, had some self esteem, some self worth."

But that was the easy way out and not what Pattie wanted. Neither did Kyle. The two went through counseling.

"All of it required a lot of work. The easiest thing would have been for both of us to walk away from it. I think that is why a lot of marriages fail today, because the easy thing is to walk away and say, 'I don't need this in my life.' But we said 'I do' through good times and bad times. We had made the commitment to each other and to those children. I remember telling a friend one night, 'If I leave, where does that leave Adam? He won't be able to pursue what he wants to pursue.' Adam was clear that

racing was what he wanted to do. Not just Adam, but all of those kids thought their daddy hung the moon. I couldn't dispel that."

Pattie also knew Kyle well enough to know that this was not the Kyle she fell in love with and married. This was a Kyle who had let the pressures of the business take over his life.

"I was raised to be a compassionate person, to be a loving person, to see the Lord in all things. When I look at Kyle, I can't carry his bags. I am working very, very hard to be that kind of person. He makes everyone feel special just to be around him, he always has. He has passed those qualities on to our kids. I see it every day. Like with the Hole in the Wall Gang camp. That is Kyle. I'm just the tool going out there to the meetings because he can't be there. I think in my heart that I am doing these things for all the right reasons, all of the sick kids, but there is a part of me that thinks this can be a good thing for Kyle Petty. This can make Kyle happy."

Given everything the family went through in 2000, it would seem that peace or happiness is an impossibility.

Just a couple of months before his death, as Adam was preparing to qualify for his first-ever Winston Cup start on March 31, 2000, at Texas Motor Speedway, Pattie talked a bit about wrecks and how one deals with them as the wife, and now mother, of a driver.

"All you can do is watch and pray," she says. "It is a helpless feeling. You learn, though, that when you are in a helpless position, what you do doesn't make or break it. You just wait, that's all you can do."

Now, despite her incredible loss, her attitude on that front has changed little.

"That is what they are going to do whether we pitch a fit about it or not. We trust the Lord, give them our blessings, and pray for them. That's all we can do. I did that for Adam and the ultimate accident happened. I never once had any blame for anyone where Adam was concerned. It was an accident. That's the only way we can look at it.

"I panic when Austin is in the Durango and drives out the driveway. That horrifies me more than him getting in a race car.

"I don't think about Kyle getting hurt. I want him to win. I want him to come back when the race is over with a smile on his face. So I think that more than being nervous and more than being fretful about him getting hurt, or worse, I get very anxious for him to do well.

"I've learned over the last few months that you just trust in the Lord in all things, and that is all you can do."

Buffy Waltrip

The tears were beginning to flow but Buffy Waltrip made no attempt to stop them. These were tears of joy that had been pent up for years. The fairy tale she and her husband, Michael, had been living for the past five months was about to reach the ultimate climax.

After 462 tries, Michael was en route to winning a Winston Cup race. And that first trip to victory lane was about to come in the biggest race of them all—the 2001 Daytona 500. Older brother Darrell, who knows the indescribable joy of winning NASCAR's greatest race, was in the broadcast booth calling the final laps for Fox Television's inaugural telecast. He made few futile attempts at containing his excitement during the final laps.

"Hold on, Michael. Hold on, Michael," he urged during the final lap before bursting into celebration. "Michael Waltrip is going to win the Daytona 500!"

Down on the pit box, Buffy watched him lead the freight train through the dogleg on the front stretch and then buried her head in her hands as he took them through turns 1 and 2 and down the backstretch. "I was just praying he wouldn't get into a wreck or that I wouldn't hear the spotter come on the radio and say, 'OK, they're coming by on the outside.'"

She never heard those words. As waves of emotion began to take control, many of the feelings that overtook her were very foreign, and oddly enough, a bit unsettling. "I was more comfortable with pulling for him to finish 20th. I was used to that. Don't get me wrong, it was a great feeling, but it was a really strange feeling.

"I think I was in shock [when I got to victory lane]. You feel kind of numb for a while when something that large happens."

Opposite: Buffy was right there through the years when Michael was constantly asked when he would win a points race. (He had won The Winston all-star race in 1996, but that event does not count as a regular points-paying NASCAR victory). To her it didn't matter, but as Michael's winless streak extended, the joy of racing diminished for them both. (Steven Rose/MMP, Inc.)

The event was Michael's first behind the wheel of the No. 15 NAPA Chevrolet and driving for car owner Dale Earnhardt. That union had been one that Michael and Buffy had dreamed of for years and was finally formed in September of 2000. It was time for Michael to win a race, and Earnhardt was the one who knew he could do it.

The champagne and Gatorade showers were flowing in victory lane, but it didn't take long for Michael and Buffy to want Dale and Teresa to arrive and share in the celebration. After all, this was their triumph too. They anxiously awaited the sight of Earnhardt parting the sea of people and grabbing Waltrip by the shoulder.

That hand on the shoulder never came.

"I knew there had been a wreck [on the last lap]," Buffy says. "But I don't know if I even knew it was Dale until we got to victory lane and Ty [Norris, general manager of Dale Earnhardt, Inc.] told us he was in the wreck, but we still had no idea how serious."

On the final lap, as Michael took the checkered flag with Dale Earnhardt Jr. close behind, Earnhardt was being swept up in a turn-4 melee. As the victory celebration continued without their car owners and best friends, Buffy assumed that Dale had been taken to the infield care center—standard procedure following a wreck. Then Ken Schrader showed up. Schrader wasn't supposed to be in victory lane. Ken and Michael had a deal that when Michael won his first race, Ken wouldn't go to victory lane, he would be planning the party.

"What are you doing here?" Michael said. "You are supposed to be getting the party going."

Ken pulled Michael close and told him Dale had been in a wreck and it was not good. He had been the first person to get to Dale's car after the accident. Still, the Waltrips refused to believe that "not good" could mean not alive. They carried on with photos and then proceeded to the press box and began the post-race media frenzy. Once Michael was situated behind the podium, their public relations representative, Brooke Mitchell, telephoned the Richard Childress Racing team doctor. As Michael fielded questions, Buffy's eyes never left Brooke. After just a few minutes she hung up the phone, turned to the speedway PR director, and motioned across her neck for him to cut the press conference. "We've got to go," Brooke said.

It was then that Buffy's heart began to pound. "I could tell when she hung up the phone something wasn't right. We hadn't been there that long, especially for someone who just won his first race and it's the Daytona 500."

They were led to the elevator. Everyone was kept out except for the van driver and Brooke. Brooke broke the news that Dale had died.

Buffy was gripped with a pain she could never have imagined feeling when she first met Michael during her carefree college days.

Elizabeth "Buffy" Franks first met Michael when she was earning a degree in business at the University of North Carolina–Charlotte. During college she worked as a waitress at Sandwich Construction Co., a popular area hang out, which at the time was also a retreat for the race teams whose shops were then concentrated in Harrisburg, just minutes from Lowe's Motor Speedway.

"I knew all these guys in racing. They were all my buddies when I came into work and they were fun and really cool, but when I left work that was it. That was my only relationship with any of them or with racing at that time. I was totally into college. I liked going to fraternity parties and hanging out with my college friends."

Michael was one of those whom she laughed and joked with at Sandwich Construction Co. But upon earning her business degree from UNCC, her focus was on her career. She intended to use her business mind and pursue a career in marketing. It wasn't until she began working for a motorsports souvenir and marketing company that Michael began his efforts to woo her.

"It was the unknown that bothered me," Buffy says. "I didn't know

• • •

what these guys were like other than the way they acted at the restaurant. What I thought I knew bothered me. To me, they were wild race car drivers. That whole scene bothered me. I had a job in racing and I really liked my job. That also made me a little nervous about getting involved with a driver."

Despite the fact that she found the guys fun and charming to serve food and drinks to, Buffy still had visions of a wild party scene beyond the doors of the restaurant. "I had pictures in my head of the trophy girls and all of that."

But Buffy possesses the kind of beauty and style suitable for the pages of *Vogue* magazine, long legs and an infectious smile, all of which kept Michael from giving up easily. His persistence eventually paid off.

"He was sweet about it and romantic about it. He wasn't going to give up, but he did it on my terms and he did it at my pace, and that just kind of won my heart after several months. He would leave notes on my car, send me flowers or little cards."

Finally during Michigan race weekend in August 1992, she agreed to go to dinner with Michael and Dale and Kelley Jarrett. "I had to leave the track early to take a sponsor to the airport and then I went back to the Hampton Inn, where I was staying, to wait for Michael to call."

But the phone never rang. "I kept thinking, 'My goodness, he has been asking me out for months and I finally say yes and he stands me up!'"

Buffy was on her way out the door, en route to McDonald's, when the phone rang. She was informed Michael had had an accident during qualifying and was at Foote Hospital.

Along with giving him a concussion, the impact had caused Michael to bite through his lower lip and it was going to require several stitches. He was completely alone when Buffy arrived. The situation was a bit awkward—she didn't feel like she knew Michael very well, at least not well enough to know what he expected of her in such a situation. Yet when the doctors arrived to stitch up his lip, he wanted her to hold his hand. "I fell in love with him at that moment.

"It was that vulnerability. Maybe that was the Lord's way of opening up my heart so that I could see that side of him. The side I had seen before was the professional race car driver and playboy."

It didn't take long for things to become serious between them. Buffy began traveling with Michael every weekend, which meant her own career stalled. She quit her job to be with Michael at the racetrack every week. There were aspects of the situation that made the transition easy. "I felt needed and wanted all of the time. Here was this guy, he had been a bachelor for his entire racing career. He always traveled alone and now he wanted me with him all of the time. I felt a real need there. I helped him with fan mail. I would go over contracts with him. I guess because I felt so needed and involved in his business it was kind of natural for me to give up my career."

But Buffy still sought the reassurance of her father, Bev.

"My father gave me great advice. He said, 'If you need to do this to take this relationship to the next level then do it, but be true to yourself and if time passes and the relationship is not going where you think it should or it doesn't feel right, then be true to yourself and go back to your goals.'"

Those words gave Buffy the security to know that at age 24 she could do this, and if it didn't work out and a year or so down the road and she had to return to the life she gave up, she could. She would always have her degree and her brain.

Traveling with Michael and becoming involved in his life also meant she was a part of the many dinners with sponsors and car owners, something that became unexpectedly difficult.

"It was hard for me because when you are just a girlfriend, no matter how serious the relationship, you are only going to get a certain amount of respect in business-dinner situations and we were constantly in that situation. It bothered me."

A girlfriend is never afforded the same respect as a wife. When people discovered that Buffy no longer worked so that she could travel with Michael full time, she often felt looked down upon. "I'm not sure how to describe it. I don't know if it is because people aren't sure you are going to be around from week to week until you get married or engaged. I don't know, but there is a sort of a stigma to the girlfriend thing." She felt somehow that it was not OK to the outside world for her to allow Michael to support her until she became Mrs. Michael Waltrip.

So by the time the 1993 season began, it was time to talk marriage. While Michael had no objections to marrying Buffy, in fact he wanted to, he didn't want to discuss it.

Buffy explains: "We all come to the table with this preconceived fairy tale notion of what getting married and being married is going to be like. In his mind, I think his thoughts were that he would secretly go out and buy me a ring and propose and it would be a total shock and I would be real excited. Well, I wasn't expecting it to happen like that. I think it is OK, even important, to talk about this subject and have that line of communication open."

Michael did manage to go out and secretly purchase the ring, turning down a golf invitation to spend an afternoon at a jeweler. He carried it around in his briefcase, waiting for just the right moment to pop the question. That moment finally arrived, but it wasn't how he expected it.

On April 2, 1993, Michael won the Busch Series race at Bristol. The win was especially emotional because defending Winston Cup champion Alan Kulwicki had been killed in a plane crash near Blountville, Tennessee, the night before. Michael, like the rest of the racing community, was devastated. Without hesitation he dedicated the win to Alan. With emotions running high in victory lane, he grabbed Buffy, pulled her to his side, and began to introduce her on national television.

"Here's my girlfriend, Buffy, who I plan to marry someday."

Buffy smiled, not really focusing on the words Michael had just said. "I remember thinking, 'Well, that's sweet, he's trying to make sure people give me a little more respect. He wants everyone to know he loves me.'"

"You will marry me one day, won't you?" Michael asked again, on camera.

"Yeah," Buffy said, still unaware that this was an actual proposal.

Max Helton, of Motor Racing Outreach, was standing nearby and heard him. "Did you just ask her to marry you?"

"Yes," Michael said, and turned to Buffy. "The ring is in the truck."

The couple married in November 1993. They had a little girl together, Margaret Carol (nicknamed "Macy"), in September 1997.

Because Buffy had already been traveling with Michael before they married, the rigors of the Winston Cup schedule and life on the road were not new to her. Still, this was never the life she had imagined for herself. She had always envisioned a career of her own that put her business/marketing degree to use. She'd planned to have a nine-to-five life, with a regular job, much like the life many of her college friends are currently living. But Buffy's childhood involved a lot of moving around, and she credits the conditioning she got as a youngster for making it so easy for her to adapt to a 36-race, cross-country schedule.

By the time Buffy entered the fifth grade, she had attended four different elementary schools. Her father, Bev, worked for Georgia Pacific, and when the opportunities for promotions came up he never passed. He transitioned from engineering, to sales, to management, and then into upper management, all the while moving his family from Louisiana, to Michigan, and then to North Carolina.

"My dad is so driven and so goal oriented. Some people might criticize the fact that he moved his family around so much. It was hard. But any time life poses challenges like that, they are hard in the moment, but then you look back and see that challenges make you grow."

When the family moved to Asheboro, North Carolina, in the middle of her high school years, Buffy found it very difficult to find acceptance. "I had been an athlete and a cheerleader and on student council in Michigan, and all of a sudden I'm at a new school and they already have all their cheerleaders and athletes and student council. So for me to butt in and try to get involved in all that … a lot of people were resentful. It was very challenging."

Buffy used some of the drive and determination she learned from her father to make things work for her.

"They didn't have any other girls running cross country. [My junior year] I was the only girl, so I would train every day with all the guys, but then when we would go to compete, other schools had girls. So I would race against other girls, but I had to train with the guys. The next year more girls came out." And the girls cross-country team at Asheboro High School has blossomed into a solid program today.

Her running also had an effect on her husband. Michael started running with Buffy, who enjoyed running three to five miles a day. She says she has "never once in my life wanted to run a marathon. If you know a little bit about running, you've got to know that marathon runners are crazy."

Michael competed in, and finished, three marathons in less than twelve months, including the famed Boston Marathon in 2000.

Michael Waltrip, at 6 foot 5 inches and 220 pounds, doesn't have the ideal body type for a long-distance runner, and his training regimen has to be built around his race schedule. Buffy, on the other hand, is petite and leggy, so running has always come naturally to her. Still, 26.2 miles was less than appealing. Boston didn't offer a half-marathon, but when Michael competed at Kiawah Island and Tampa, Buffy ran the half at each. "Now, those are great!" Buffy says. "When I ran my first one I said I was going to do it in 2 hours and I did it in 2 hours. So I should have set a better goal. My next one I did in 1 hour, 48 minutes. So I knocked quite a bit off." That is an average of 8:24 per mile for 13.1 miles—an impressive pace.

Despite the physical toll, those races were fun for both of them, something that was becoming increasingly rare in their other racing life. During the late '90s the joy was gradually being sucked out of their weekly trip to the track.

Before the 2001 Daytona 500 win, the question never stopped coming: When is

Michael going to win a race? He'd made 462 tries and had zero wins. In 1996 Michael did win The Winston, a non-points all-star race, and he had to beat the best to do it, including Earnhardt, Dale Jarrett, Bobby Labonte, and Rusty Wallace. But because it did not count in the championship chase, in the eyes of the critics it didn't count much at all. Buffy watched as Michael answered with a joke and a smile, knowing that all the while, his belief in himself was being chiseled away.

"We would have moments, days, weeks where our spirit was hurt and we were all down. But we would always seem to pull through," she says. "Somehow the good always outweighed the bad.

For me, I focused on the people rather than the racing. The friendships were, and are, very important to me, and those were the things that mattered."

It was one of the most important friendships the couple had made that led Michael to answer that lingering question. Dale and Teresa Earnhardt and Michael and Buffy had started doing things together frequently after Michael and Buffy began dating. Michael and Buffy were often invited to join Dale and Teresa on their boat in the Bahamas to relax on off weekends. "It's hard sometimes with other couples—maybe the men get along great, but you don't have a lot in common with the wife. But with us, we all got along really well and just really enjoyed each other's company."

Dale had always believed in Michael's ability to drive a race car. The pair had talked for years about the possibility of working together, when finally in September 2000, the talk became reality.

"[DEI] was the opportunity. Next to giving birth to Macy, it was the single most exciting thing that had happened in our relationship.

"For five months our life was just a fairy tale. We were already very thankful that we had wonderful families, a beautiful home, a wonderful child together, but his racing career was always more of a negative. But all of a sudden everything was perfect. It was no longer a negative thing to think about racing. We were actually excited about January [2001] testing."

January testing seems a lifetime ago now. She swallows hard and tries to recall just how happy those times were, and how dreadfully quickly it can all change.

"We went from being on cloud nine to basically being in hell.

"It is hard to not feel a knife jabbing your heart at some point every day.

"Sometimes when something is bigger than you can imagine handling, the best thing is to take it one day at a time. Losing Dale is a situation that was much bigger than we were prepared to handle. So you just have to wake up each day and try real hard to be as positive as you can that day and deal with what comes your way on that day. Then get up the next day and do it again and hope that each day becomes a little easier."

STEVIE WALTRIP

The year was 1983. Stevie Waltrip walked up to the garage gate at Pocono Raceway.

"You cannot come in here," the guard said. Women were not allowed.

Stevie didn't even want to go in the garage, but at Pocono, the only way to get to pit road was through the garage. "We were driving for Junior Johnson then. I had been keeping gas mileage and laps for Darrell all through the '70s. So I had been at this fight for a long time.

"I don't see myself as a strong, forceful person, but I am stubborn, and when something doesn't make sense to me, I will die trying to make it different."

Breaking new ground was not what Stevie had intended. Her goal was simple: Darrell wanted her to keep laps for him during the race. He liked having her on pit road. She needed access to pit road. Simple as that.

"It gave me a purpose, it was helpful for him."

Each year NASCAR was willing to sell Stevie a license. The trouble was the gate guards didn't always know, or care, who she was, and she wasn't getting in.

"I didn't even try to get into the garage area for years and years and years. I didn't have a reason to, but there were times when something legitimate would come up and I would need to speak to Darrell. I would have to go to the NASCAR box, that little house by the garage entrance, and they would page Darrell over the loudspeaker. Well, there's practice going on. I mean, come on, you can't hear a page in the garage area. So that never worked.

"Then I would stand there and hope I saw someone that I knew who could possibly go to the truck or car and tell Darrell that I was at the gate, could he please come over. That is how we communicated at the racetrack."

Opposite: Darrell's retirement came about a decade later than Stevie had expected, and although he is not driving, his work for FOX Sports in the broadcast booth keeps the pair close to the track and their racing family. (Steven Rose/MMP Inc.)

Stevie looked over into the garage area at Pocono and saw some people "who I think were guests of Winston, but they were men and they were women and they had suits on and the woman had their high heels on and skirts, very nicely dressed. I'm thinking, why are they allowed in there and why am I not?"

By now her mood matched her fiery red hair.

She went to a NASCAR official who regularly signed everyone in. He knew who Stevie was and he knew what she needed, but on this day he wasn't going to help. That left Stevie with just one option.

"I told the official OK, and I walked to the gate and I kept on walking. The guard at the gate started yelling at me, then he and some of the other guards grabbed at me and I just kept going. I was so mad. All I could think was, I'm just trying to do what I'm supposed to do every race day."

She had no idea how much commotion she caused, she only knew that she had a job to do and she was simply trying to do it. And she would do it again the next week and the one after that and the one after that. NASCAR heard about the incident and Stevie got a call from one of the officials, asking what they could do.

"The wives need access. The wives need a permanent credential. We need to be able to go anywhere we need to go without being harassed by a guard."

Shortly after that, in 1984, things changed, and wives were permitted unobstructed access.

"I'd like to say I had that all planned out. If Darrell hadn't been running well at the time, nobody probably would have noticed. The Lord would have used somebody else to make that happen. I was just trying to do what I needed to do and what Darrell needed me to do. I'm not a pioneer. That is not who I am."

Who Stevie is has nearly everything to do with the influence of her grandparents. In her eyes, her grandparents hung the moon.

"My dad's parents were my two favorite people on this earth. I adored them," Stevie's eyes light up and she looks into the distance as she remembers them. It has been a long time since she has shared these thoughts with anyone. "My grandfather was a professor at Southern Methodist University in Texas. He taught economics and Spanish. My dream was that I would go to SMU and live with my grandmother and my grandfather and sleep in the room where my dad grew up. That was my dream. I wanted to teach like my grandfather did. I adored them."

The day before Thanksgiving in 1965, Stevie's grandparents were in an automobile accident. Her grandfather was killed almost instantly and her grandmother died four days later. At 15, Stevie's entire world was turned upside down in the blink of an eye.

Then she met Darrell.

They met at her best friend's wedding rehearsal. Stevie was 16 and Darrell was 19, and at that time, "that was much older." Dating in the conventional sense was pretty much out of the question, but developing a friendship wasn't.

"We would ride around in the car together. We would go get a Coke. We'd laugh. But it was never a date. He never called me and asked me out and he never came to the house and picked me up."

Still reeling from her grandparents' death, Stevie was desperately seeking some peace for herself. She chose Holton Arms, a boarding school in Washington D.C., thinking the distance might bring her solace and comfort.

"I should never have done that. It was my idea. My parents didn't send me. I was the least academic of anybody in my family, but because my grandparents' death affected me so adversely, I just wanted something different. I wanted to run away, and I did."

Stevie didn't fit the mold of a Holton Arms lady. She laughs at the thought of it. "I just wanted to have fun. I didn't want to study. I couldn't have cared less about any of it. I really wasted two years of my life."

The school asked her not to return for her senior year. So it was back to Owensboro, Kentucky. Stevie and Darrell had written and talked while she was away at school, and had spent time together during the summer. They were destined for more when she returned home.

"There was something there from the time I met him until right now. I don't think at 16 I would call it love. There was just an attraction there, and it evolved into love."

They had their first official date that fall and married the following August, much to the chagrin of her family.

"That was a terrible year [1969]. It was awful. We tried to elope and got caught. My dad even pretended to have a heart attack to slow us down," she says matter-of-factly, as if every dad has done the same thing. "I look back now … my mom and dad were right, we should not have gotten married when we got married. I know I married who I was supposed to marry and he knows he married who he was supposed to marry. We are soul mates. But we should not have gotten married that year. I should have gone on to SMU and he should have done some more growing up."

Once Stevie's parents realized there was no stopping them, they supported the marriage. "They knew they could influence us in a positive or negative way depending on

Opposite: Stevie's job in Darrell's pit was to time his laps and help estimate fuel mileage. (Steven Rose/MMP Inc.)

how they handled it. Actually, my dad became one of Darrell's best friends. [Darrell] has always said if he and I ever had any problems and one wanted to go one way and one the other, he would go home to my parents."

It wasn't long after they were married that they made the move to Franklin, Tennessee, so Darrell could race every week.

"I don't think he was even getting a salary. He got a percentage of whatever he won, and he won a lot. He won enough so that we could pay our rent and eat and have gas money to get to the races the next week, and that was about all we had. So that is how we lived for five or six years."

Before they left Owensboro, Stevie had put in two semesters at Kentucky Wesleyan; and earning that college degree was very important to her.

"Racing was what Darrell did. It was how he was going to support us. I just wanted a college degree for myself and in case [racing] didn't work out, if I needed to go to work, I needed a degree to do that."

She enrolled in Peabody—a part of Vanderbilt in Nashville—and began a five-year program to get her degree in special education and elementary education. But as

Darrell's career grew, Stevie's five-year program became a six-year program. "I would schedule my classes on Monday, Tuesday, Wednesday, and Thursday so that I could go to the racetrack with Darrell on the weekends. At the time we didn't have a plane, so Darrell would drive me back on Sunday nights after the race so that I could make my eight o'clock class on Monday morning.

"It was as important to Darrell as it was to me for me to get my degree. That was just part of who he saw me as. I get a lot of credit, and I deserve a lot of credit, for being as supportive and encouraging as I have been to Darrell through the years, but when you look at things like that, he's been equally so for me."

In 1976, all Stevie had left to do was a semester of student teaching and she'd have her degree. "But because I had to be there Monday, Tuesday, Wednesday, Thursday, and Friday, I ran into problems. I couldn't be there on Friday and they weren't going to budge on that."

Stevie was OK with it. To her, she had accomplished quite a bit and it had not been easy. But that wasn't good enough for Darrell. In 1981, his first year driving for Junior Johnson, Darrell worked it out so that she could do her student teaching. Now Stevie was able to teach on Friday, and then fly to the racetrack

for the weekend and fly home Sunday night.

"I'm so glad I did it. I couldn't care less about a masters or a doctorate or whatever. I just wanted my one little degree and I'm satisfied," she smiles proudly, knowing deep down just how tremendous her accomplishment is in conjunction with a demanding race schedule.

That degree came in handy when she and Darrell made the decision to homeschool their two daughters. It was a logical choice, because they wanted to be able to travel together as a family all the time.

Upon meeting her children, it is clear that the girls are not just absorbing the proper book lessons. You would be hard pressed to find anyone with better manners than the Waltrip girls. They are expecting guests for this evening's Winston Cup race at Bristol— the 2000 goracing.com 500. "Happy Hour" practice is still going on under the late after-noon hot August sun. Yet Stevie sits relaxed in the cool comfort of her motor home while Jessica, less than a month from her 13th birthday, willingly escorts her younger sister to and from a friend's motor home. When the phone rings to announce their friends' arrival, Stevie answers the phone, but it is Jessica who unhesitatingly goes out and gets them. To those who watched her grow from the curly-haired girl by her daddy's side to the teen she is now, it is easy to see the influence her mother has had.

"She is 13 going on 30," Stevie smiles. Stevie may not have thought of herself as a lady at that age, but Jessica definitely is.

"Jessica has never been in a public or a private school. I think it has really worked for our family. Darrell helps me a lot. He helped me a lot with Sarah Caitlyn last year [first grade]. He did the science, the Bible, and history and I did math and reading with her. That helped so much. As Jessica has gotten older, the more we have had to stay home so that she can be involved in the things other kids are involved in. She loves basketball. Next year [2001], we'll only go to about half the races, so we'll pick and choose and get more involved with the community at home [in Tennessee]."

Having children was something Darrell and Stevie had always wanted to do. It was part of their plan, and both were taken a bit by surprise when the process was anything but simple.

"We didn't know we had any problems, so we were trying to have children years before we ever got to have children." In fact, Stevie had two miscarriages and she believes she had a third; "it was very early on in that one."

But in 1985, Stevie got pregnant again. The pregnancy was monitored constantly by a physician and Stevie and Darrell began to feel like they were going to be parents.

"We were so excited. We were in Daytona. All four of our parents were there. So we told them they were going to be grandparents."

Their parents were in a state of joyous disbelief, thoroughly convinced that they were joking since they had already been married for 16 years and had not yet had children. After breaking the news to the family, there was no stopping Darrell. He won the IROC race at Daytona, and upon entering the press box for his post-race interviews, Darrell said, "I don't want to talk about that. I want to tell you all that I'm going to be a daddy."

But Darrell's excitement wasn't enough to ensure the pregnancy would make it to term. Stevie pauses, "That baby went to heaven."

After that it was difficult for the two to even keep trying. Doctors were telling them that Stevie would need to have major surgery, and even then she might not be able to carry a child to term if she got pregnant again. Neither one of them wanted Stevie to go through a major surgical procedure that might be ineffective.

"We just quit doing what the doctors said and lived our lives."

They began adoption proceedings in late 1986. Darrell was going to turn 40 in February and agencies wouldn't approve an adoption if you were over 40. "So we started that whole process and I got pregnant with Jessica."

Stevie had surgery to make sure Jessica was secure in the womb and she went to the doctor every week to have an injection to keep her from going into premature labor. They finally told their families four months

into the pregnancy, but kept it fairly quiet beyond that.

Darrell was in the midst of what, up to that point, was one of his longest winless streaks ever. It had been thirteen seasons since he had gone winless for an entire season. But in 1987 he was on that path. Jessica was born September 17, 1987. The very next week, Darrell won at Martinsville.

He won one race in the spring of 1992 while Stevie was pregnant with Sarah, and then he repeated the new-daughter victory celebration with a win at Bristol in August, just four days after she was born.

Now, Darrell is just a few months away from his final race as a driver. Both he and Stevie seem to be struggling at times to find some peace with the ending.

"So we find ourselves here [in 2000], and even though this is the most painful time for us, we're OK about it." Stevie says, thinking more about the pain of what Darrell's final Winston Cup season has come to. "I miss doing well. I miss being competitive. I miss having the confidence in the race team. I miss so much for Darrell all those things that he is missing."

Between 1993 and 1996, Stevie's father succumbed to cancer, as did Darrell's, her mother had Alzheimer's, and her sister developed a brain tumor. Then in 1995 Darrell was in a wreck in the Winston—NASCAR's all-star event. Racing Dale Earnhardt for the lead, the pair collided and sparks flew. It was that wreck that Stevie believes changed Darrell's heart for the rest of his racing career.

"The things that happened with our moms and dads, those were things you expect at some point in time. You expect accidents in racing. You expect, I suppose, to be realistic, at some point in time you expect an injury. But I never expected Darrell's career to move to the place that it has moved to.

Stevie was in her early 30s when she turned to Darrell and said, "I hope you reach a point in racing so that when you quit, people will say, 'I wonder what he quit for?'"

Darrell's response was that he would probably quit when he was 40.

"Yeah, right," Stevie thought, not believing him for a minute. She was correct.

Darrell was 53 when he drove his final Winston Cup race at Atlanta Motor

• • •

Speedway in November 2000. Instead of people wondering why he quit, they have spent many of the last several years wondering why he hadn't. It got to the point that even Darrell, on his final day, a chilly Monday in front of half-filled stands at Atlanta Motor Speedway after Sunday's event had been rained out, may have wished he had hung it up a bit sooner.

"I feel like I have been married to two different men with the same name, and I have. He is a completely different human being than the man that I married. I think outwardly he is. Inwardly there was the something I always saw in him that I see in him now, but I think I was the only one. He is a good man.

"I don't know what to expect [from retirement]. I don't like change. What's familiar, even though it's painful, is easier for me to deal with than the unfamiliar.

"This process that we are in right now is the hardest because it came so unexpectedly. But I wouldn't take anything for it, because I know that we have become better … you can't go through pain and not be changed by it, and we are changed for the better."

In early August of 2000, Darrell and Stevie Waltrip bought some land on a lake near their home in Tennessee.

The fact that they purchased some undeveloped land to build a cabin on, or simply enjoy nature on, is remarkable, because this land's only purpose is relaxation and family fun—no race shop, no race cars, no race anything.

"We have never bought anything of any significance, other than our home, that didn't have anything to do with racing.

"We've bought race cars. We've bought race teams. We've bought airplanes so that we can get to the races. We've bought buses so that we can live at the racetrack, but we have never bought anything that had to do with fun. So we are going to learn to have some fun and I'm not sure what that is."

Left: **A Waltrip family portrait, 2000.**
(Steven Rose/MMP Inc.)

DEB WILLIAMS

From the time Deb Williams was born until just past her first birthday, she was a typical infant who spent a solid amount of time crying. There was only one method her parents could find that would curtail that crying and lull her to sleep: a trip to the infield at Asheville-Weaverville dirt track.

"My first memory of life is a stock car race," Deb says. "I remember sitting on the trunk of Mom and Dad's car above turns 1 and 2 at Asheville-Weaverville when it was a dirt track."

Since her older sister, Gail, had no interest in cars or sports, Deb got to play son and daughter to her father.

"I grew up hanging out with my daddy around garages. He loved automobiles. In Clanton [North Carolina] there were two things—football and fast cars. I loved them both."

Deb also discovered very early on that she loved to write, and her favorite time of day was when her father read the newspaper to her and Gail.

"I used to sit around when I was 9 and write stories for fun," Deb says. "Daddy would read the newspaper to us. We would go sit on the arm of the chair and point to what we wanted him to read to us."

So it only makes sense that Deb is now the editor of *NASCAR Winston Cup Scene,* a weekly newspaper about stock car racing. She has twice been honored as the National Motorsports Press Association writer of the year, in 1990 and '94. She is the only woman to win that award twice. In 1992 she became the only woman ever to be awarded the Henry T. McClenon Award for lifetime achievement in motorsports writing.

While racing has always been in Deb's blood, she has hardly taken the conventional route to a career in sportswriting.

She decided when she was 13 that the local paper—the *Asheville Citizen*—was really doing a lousy job with its race coverage. "They had facts wrong, you name it. I decided I could do just as good a job or better." Thus her sportswriting dream was formed. During her senior year at Pisgah High School in 1972, she approached the community paper in Waynesville and expressed an interest in covering games for them.

"Well, the managing editor thought this was very interesting," Deb says. "There just weren't many females interested in covering sports back then."

The kicker was, Deb was also a majorette. That meant she had to cover the game, do the half-time show, cover the second half, do her postgame interviews, and write a story.

"I would try to have slacks and a jacket to put on after halftime, but sometimes I didn't have time, so there I would be in my majorette uniform and a raincoat, running up and down the sidelines covering the game. I had to do my own photography then, too."

Deb believed it was possible to be both a lady and a tomboy, and she was both. "You could be in pageants and be a majorette and wear evening gowns and you could be a tomboy too. My only complaint was that I couldn't walk in an evening gown. I walk with a purpose. I always told my father you couldn't get anywhere taking little steps and walking like a lady. So I simply solved the problem by hiking my skirt up above my knees. It made him so mad."

Nancy Drew mysteries were her favorites growing up, and she would devour the books in two days or less.

"So, when I was in junior high I decided I was going to be an FBI agent. That was when they didn't have female FBI agents. Criminology always intrigued me. I always

loved mysteries, man, I was always reading a Nancy Drew mystery when I was young. I think I kept that publisher in business for a long time."

Deb's love of mysteries and law enforcement stayed with her when she got to college. So she added criminology to her journalism studies. And it was in college at East Tennessee State University that she met and became engaged to a man who was going to make a career in the army, Rick Meredith. She quickly learned there were things she was supposed to do to learn how to be an officer's wife. Never one to follow the conventional path, "I thought, 'Why learn how to be an officer's wife, when I can be an officer?'"

Deb began taking courses in the military science pro-

gram. She joined the women's drill team and sponsor core and was one of the first women to pledge the military fraternity Scabbard and Blade.

"I initially went into the military science program to understand Rick's job better, but then I got into it and liked it and decided I could be an officer too. And I was good at it."

But when it came time to sign her military contract, Deb couldn't go through with it. "I still wanted to be a sportswriter and I felt that if I went into the army it would put me behind in my sports writing career. I felt that being a woman, I needed to take every opportunity that I possibly could. And if I accepted my commission for four years, that would put me four years behind in my career."

It was also her career that kept her from ultimately making the walk down the aisle with Rick Meredith.

"We were supposed to have gotten married in June of '76 and I called it off in April. He said to me that he wished it had been another man instead of my career, because he could fight another man, but he couldn't fight my career.

"I came so close to making a big mistake that would have totally altered the course of my life. I also don't think I was mature enough to be married until I was about 40."

Now 48, Deb has never married, but she has no regrets about that. "I've never been one of these people that had to get married and have children. Those things have just never been priorities in my life."

Racing always has been.

And at the time Deb was growing up, if you were into racing, you very likely were into Richard Petty.

"I was a huge Richard Petty fan. I mean I ate, slept … everything was Richard Petty when I was growing up. That is how I was known throughout junior high and high school. I had a Plymouth Racing jacket and I wore it everywhere and I always got picked on for it, but I didn't care. I even wrote my book reports about racing and race cars."

One of her high school graduation presents was a trip to the World 600 in Charlotte in May. It was that weekend that she promised herself that she would return to Charlotte as a reporter in no more than ten years.

She achieved that goal in seven years when she began covering Winston Cup racing with United Press International. While she was with UPI, her by-then good friend

Left: Deb as an infant with her mom. (Deb Williams collection)

Opposite: A 5-year-old Deb with her parents in the mountains of North Carolina. (Deb Williams collection)

•   •   •

Richard Petty reached a milestone in racing, and she felt she had also reached a pinnacle in her career.

"When Richard Petty won his 200th race on July 4, 1984, I was with UPI and I felt like it was a statement for me that I was working for an international wire news service and I was the one who got to tell the world, and all of those people that made fun of me in high school, about Richard's achievement.

"I felt like I personally had accomplished something then, too."

That moment is one of the most memorable in her racing career, but her first interview with Richard was far from it.

"Oh gosh, I was a fool.

"I wanted so much to impress him. I had admired him so much. I was so nervous, you know how you just want to make such a good impression, and you want him to think you are really intelligent and you know what you are talking about, and that you are not just some geeky female who doesn't know squat about cars.

"Well, Richard was giving us a tour of Petty Enterprises and it was January, so needless to say it was quite cold. We walked through the door and I was the last one in, but I thought Richard was going to turn around and shut the door. He turned around and looked at me and said, 'Were you raised in a barn? Shut the door.'"

Since that first interview and the many that followed, King Richard has become more than just an interview subject. Richard, his wife, Linda, and Deb have developed a tremendous friendship.

"Linda and I became very close instantly, and in '92 I was basically assigned to him since it was his last season as a driver. I was with them all the time.

"Now he treats me like a daughter."

That friendship with Linda is probably one of the factors that helped her do her job. When she began her career, women were barely tolerated in the garage area. The drivers' families weren't welcomed at that time.

"My first credential from Darlington [1979] said, 'No women in the pits.'"

So despite the fact that Deb was there to do a job and that she was very talented at that job, she was still a woman in a man's domain.

"It was difficult to gain credibility initially, because when I started out with UPI, I only covered a few races. The more races I went to, the more it helped.

"I made it a point that if I didn't have business in the garage, I didn't go into the garage. I wouldn't just go out there and stand around. I had some good people guide me, coach me, and take me under their wing. They told me how not to dress, told me where women before me had made mistakes and what had hurt their credibility.

"The fact that Richard Petty would stop and talk to me helped. I think people thought if Richard will stop and talk to her she must be OK. My friendship with Linda helped put the wives and girlfriends at ease."

As with any woman covering sports, whether it be 1983 or 2003, Deb is always asked about how hard it must be to be a woman in racing.

"First of all, if you look at yourself as being a woman then you are setting yourself up with an excuse for failure. I view myself as a motorsports writer who happens to be a female. I am not a female who is a motorsports writer."

It was a credit to what she has achieved as a writer, female or otherwise, that Ray Evernham asked her to write his story.

In 2000, then–Winston Cup crew chief Ray Evernham made the decision to leave Hendrick Motorsports and Jeff Gordon to spearhead Dodge's return to racing.

"We sat down and did the story about that and how it all came about. I could see that bringing Dodge back to racing, and his involvement in it, had the makings of a book. I mentioned to him that he ought to keep some sort of diary throughout the first season so that he could recreate it. I thought that was a story people would want to read."

Ray agreed somewhat, but said only, "OK, we'll talk about that."

Deb put the idea on the back burner and went on with other things, until one day in January 2001 when she called Ray's shop to talk about something else. His marketing person grabbed the phone.

"He told me that Ray needed to talk to me. It sounded very urgent. He said that Ray had been offered a book deal and he told the publisher that he wanted me to write it.

"Wow!

"I mean what else can you say. I still float on cloud nine. That's one of those things, when you are having a bad day, that you think about. I was so honored that he thought enough of me and my work

to make such a request.

"People ask me, 'How did you pick Ray?' I say, 'I didn't pick Ray, he picked me.'"

The Ray Evernham book came together much more quickly than her biography of Alan Kulwicki, due out in late 2003, a project she took on in 1996.

"The most difficult part of the book [about Alan] to write has been the epilogue, because the publisher wants me to recreate the night of his plane crash and my feelings, and it is really hard to go back there emotionally.

"I just about had everything done when Dale [Earnhardt] got killed. I just couldn't deal with it for a while after that."

Dale Earnhardt's death rocked the entire racing community unlike anything before it, but it was Adam Petty's death in May 2000 that caused her to consider walking away from the sport entirely.

"Everyone out here becomes like family and the Pettys and I are very close. I was at Richard and Linda's house when Kyle brought Pattie and Adam home from the hospital.

"I'd known Adam his whole life. Seeing the hurt in the Pettys, it was just very hard."

A self-described "massive pack rat," Deb still has Adam's cell phone number in her Rolodex.

"There are numbers I just can't take out of my Rolodex or Day Runner. I still have [Alan] Kulwicki's, Tim Richmond's, Davey's [Allison]. I won't ever get rid of them."

In more than two decades of reporting on racing, Deb has seen many triumphs and tragedies, but the growth of recent years has surprised even her.

"I never thought that I would see the Winston Cup Champion on NBC.

"One of the other things I find so interesting is that so many of the fans now have really been fans only since, say, 1995. They don't know who Tim Richmond was. I didn't realize how fortunate I had been to grow up when I did until NASCAR had its 50th anniversary in 1998.

"I started hearing people talking about Fireball Roberts and Joe Weatherly. They would say they wish they could have seen them race. They wished they could have seen Curtis Turner and Lee Petty. Well, I did. NASCAR was only 5 years old when I was born [1954]."

The circulation of *Winston Cup Scene* was 33,000 when she started there in 1986. Now it tops out at 140,000.

Left: Deb had wanted to be a majorette since she was a child and took three years of baton lessons. She was a member of the majorette corps at Pisgah High School, and appears at the far left in this photo. (Deb Williams collection)
Below: A recent portrait of Deb. (Deb Williams collection)
Opposite: During her sophomore year at East Tennessee State University Deb was a member of the Sponsor Corps drill team. Here the team is performing before a basketball game. That same year (1976) the team won the National Collegiate Co-ed Military Drill Team Championship. (Deb Williams collection)

"All of us at *Winston Cup Scene* have been asked for our autograph and that just amazes me. To be walking down through the grandstands and have a fan stop and want to have a picture taken with me … that is just mind-boggling."

You will rarely see Deb without either a tape recorder, stack of newspapers, or handful of radios at the racetrack. Over the years, her job as a reporter has grown to entail much more than writing.

"I write a weekly column and a minimum of three features a month," Deb says. "I also select and edit the letters we receive and act as *Scene's* representative with the fans, and I appear on various radio shows throughout our markets."

She is also responsible for the more mundane task of making sure a supply of *Scenes* gets to each of the tracks. All of *Scene's* reporters and photographers are in constant radio communication with each other throughout the weekend, and it is Deb's job to make sure those radios get to and from each destination fully charged. And Deb is the one to handle complaints from drivers, owners, or crew members if they don't like what was written about them the week before.

So you might think that at home Deb might seek refuge from racing. But even if she tried, she couldn't get away from it.

Deb spent nearly a decade searching for a house in a certain area of Concord, North Carolina, just north of Charlotte.

While she had some specific characteristics she desired in a house, the most important was an intangible that she would only know when she felt it. "I wanted to walk in the door and feel like I had come home. That is the way I felt with the house I was currently living in and I wanted that feeling again."

She was on her way to make an offer on another house when she spotted the "For Sale by Owner" sign in the yard of what would be her new home. "I pulled in the driveway and it was a beautiful spring day. It was May. As soon as I walked through the front door, I knew I was home."

Well that was just the beginning. She spent some time with the owners, and when they found out Deb writes for *Winston Cup Scene,* they decided she needed to know some details about the history of the house.

"When we first moved here, every time we had a hard rain, all these beer cans and beer bottles washed up in the yard," they told her. "This went on for two solid years before we finally found out that this house is built on the parking lot of the old Concord Speedway."

"For me to have not known what that house was built on and still be drawn to it like I was—that is one of those strange spiritual things that is out of our hands."

Humpy Wheeler came out to her house to get a soil sample when he was preparing to build the dirt track at Lowe's Motor Speedway, and Deb has since learned that the old speedway is the dirt track that was used in the opening scene of the 1973 movie *The Last American Hero,* starring Jeff Bridges.

"But maybe the greatest fact I have found out is that it was the track where Dale Earnhardt drove his very first race. I have been researching and trying to find photos and diagrams. I really want to put a history together. I feel like I've got my field of dreams and it's up to me to preserve the history of it. I had been looking at that [other housing] development since the '80s and was literally hours away from ending my search when I found that house. It was meant to be."

Below: Deb has been a regular on the Kyle Petty Charity ride since it was created. (Deb Williams collection)